SEEING BIRMINGHAM BY TRAM

VOLUME II

In Loving Memory

OF THE

BIRMINGHAM
STEAM TRAMS,

WHICH SUCCUMBED ON DEC. 31ST, 1906,
TO AN ELECTRIC SHOCK.

AGED 24 YEARS.

Although perhaps shunted into the siding of 'damned with faint praise,' twenty-four years constitutes a good tour of duty. A number of publishers issued *In Memoriam* postcards making use of the electric shock quip.

SEEING BIRMINGHAM BY TRAM

VOLUME II

Eric Armstrong

The
History
Press

A typical inner-city scene from half a century ago; a bus, a tram, a gasometer, a cinema, extensive areas of sturdy stone cobbles and roadworks. The building fronted by columns is the Delicia, opened in 1923. Atypically, the tram is on its final run on 4 July 1953 when the tram service in Birmingham came to an end. This area, Gosta Green, became the site of the University of Aston, which retained the Delicia building as an arts centre.

First published 2010

The History Press
The Mill, Brimscombe Port
Stroud, Gloucestershire, GL5 2QG
www.thehistorypress.co.uk

British Library Cataloguing in Publication Data.
A catalogue record for this book is available from the British Library.

ISBN 978 0 7524 5392 7

Typesetting and origination by The History Press
Printed in Great Britain
Manufacturing managed by Jellyfish Print Solutions Ltd

CONTENTS

ACKNOWLEDGEMENTS

In carrying out the research required for this book I warmly acknowledge the help that I have received from the following sources: Bunce, J.T. et al, *History of the Corporation of Birmingham* (Birmingham Corporation); Clegg, Chris and Rosemary, *The Dream Palaces of Birmingham* (Chris and Rosemary Clegg, 1983); Collins, Paul, *Birmingham Corporation Transport 1904-1939* (Ian Allan Publishing, 1999) – *Birmingham Corporation Transport 1939-1969* (Ian Allan Publishing 1999); Harvey, David, *Birmingham in the Age of the Tram, The Eastern and Western Routes* (Silver Link Publishing, 2003) – *Birmingham in the Age of the Tram, The South-Eastern and Northern Routes* (Silver Link Publishing 2004) – *Birmingham in the Age of the Tram, The South-Western Routes* (Silver Link Publishing 2004); Jones, Douglas V., *The Story of Erdington* (The Westwood Press, 1995); Price, Victor J. *Handsworth Remembered* (Brewin Books, 1992); Alan Godfrey, various copies of old Ordnance Survey maps. Also, my thanks to a number of photographer/tram enthusiasts, principally W.A. Camwell.

INTRODUCTION

Remember Judy Garland? This may seem an odd question to raise at the start of a book about Birmingham trams but the question's relevance will soon become clear. When Judy was a young 'mega' film star, she scored a worldwide hit with a catchy song in the film musical *Meet Me in St Louis*. Some readers may remember:

Clang, clang, clang went the trolley
Ding, ding, ding went the bell
Zing, zing, zing went my heartstrings . . .
(*The Trolley Song*)

But romantic associations finish here.

For trolleys read trams. San Francisco trolleys belonged to the type in which Birmingham engineers took a close interest before recommending to a Corporation committee that cable cars should be tried out on some Birmingham streets. But more on this later.

Perhaps objects as well as locations can convey a distinctive ambience, and from my personal experience as a seasoned tram passenger, here is my stab at describing the 'nature' of the tram. Tram cars, especially those of later design, in their fine, distinctive livery of primrose yellow and dark blue, appeared pleasingly elegant, being harmoniously designed with front and back identically rounded. Their wooden interiors served as highly polished showcases for the skills of carpenters and joiners, painters and varnishers. Superlative high gloss work was carried out on doors, honey-coloured side panels and ceilings, pleasing to the eye and to the touch. No unpleasant residual whiff of petrol or diesel fumes lingered in the air. Though not soundless, trams were not noisy, just gliding and swishing along, smooth metal on smooth metal in the disciplined manner determined by the rails.

From above might be heard occasional subdued crackles accompanying the sharp blue flashes of electric blue light from the pulley heads when taking power from the overhead wiring. Muffled metallic ratcheting sounds might be heard from the vestibule where the driver (motorman) applied his skills. A man apart, the driver, standing alert and alone in his rounded cubicle, partly open to the elements on older trams. In one hand a brass, swans-neck brake handle, and in the other a shorter power control handle, both firmly held and moved according to changing needs and circumstances.

As for the conductor, he was a man of the people. In continuous contact with passengers, his job was to be sociable and good humoured at all times, if possible, while taking fares in grubby old copper coinage,

Apparently this is a South Staffs steam tram, which suggests it is close to Birmingham. Pedestrians seem only mildly interested in the passing show being photographed. The crewman dutifully keeps his eye on the road. The ladies being sheltered in the top-deck 'saloon' are not afraid to wear what appear to be straw hats or boaters.

punching and issuing tickets, giving change, all the while carrying a leather satchel which became steadily heavier as the journey progressed, and... calling out quasi orders in the style of jaunty requests:

'Hold tight!'
'Fares please!'
'Pass along the car, please, pass along the car.'

Because of its familiarity, that last plea passed into wider usage. The public were used to standing in queues – for a football match, the theatre, the cinema, wartime and post-war rations. In trams, standing passengers in the lower saloon would usually comply in good humoured fashion. The untidy line would shuffle a little nearer to the driver shielded in his cab. The vast majority of passengers would never have dreamt of pulling to one side the heavy sliding door in order to voice comment or complaint to the man at the controls.

Apart from the occasional lurch or sway, trams proceeded on their calm course in a stable, serene manner. However, stretches of the Bristol Road route allowed a sprightly driver to 'put his foot down', arousing tremors of alarm – genuine or feigned – in more nervous passengers. But from a distance and along tree-lined reservations trams could look dignified, even stately, as they glided to and fro.

Arguably, the one jarring aspect of their appearance lay in the amount and quality of the commercial advertising trams carried. Most of the adverts possessed little or no artistic merit, just presenting plain facts and clear claims from, for example – Nestles Milk, Beecham's Pills, the Beehive or a Birmingham store. But as the Corporation's aim was to operate the tramway system at a profit, the advertising revenue, arranged by a London agent, made a useful contribution to income.

For the first quarter of the twentieth century trams constituted the main workhorses of the public road transport system, but Corporation buses eventually replaced them completely.

Given what has gone before, it seems appropriate to introduce a brief background history of what happened during the years illustrated in this book. In 1948, just three years after the end of the Second World War, Birmingham Corporation published a brochure titled *Birmingham City Transport: A Cavalcade of Progress (1868-1948)*. Although some justified self-congratulation can be detected, the facts of the cavalcade come directly from the horse's mouth, hence the use of this brochure as a major source of a basic history of Birmingham trams.

Why start at 1868? Because this year brought the formation of the General Omnibus Co. which ran a fleet of horse buses from High Street to various suburbs. The remaining years of that century are marked by an intricate, baffling mesh of private companies, with the Corporation owning, leasing and managing transport systems. Suffice it to say that the first horse tram in the city plodded into service in 1872, operating between Hockley Brook and Dudley Port. It became the Corporation's practice to build and maintain the tramway tracks and to lease these out for varying periods of time to a variety of private companies, part of the intricate mesh mentioned above.

For roughly ten years horses had the rails of 4ft 8½in gauge to themselves. And then, in 1882, mechanical power in the form of the steam tram pioneered a 'noisome' course between the Old Square in the town centre and Aston – 'noisome', a carefully chosen word, being a literary adjective meaning harmful, noxious, evil-smelling, objectionable and offensive. For some, passengers and pedestrians alike, and probably crew, each of the above boxes could be ticked. But with its reduced gauge of 3ft 6in, a legal requirement due to the narrowness of some city streets, more and more track was laid and more routes opened. The Birmingham Central Tramways Co. Ltd became a major player in the tramway 'stakes', supplemented by some companies with horse buses.

Despite its relative unpopularity, quite some time elapsed before the steam tram faced competition from a viable alternative traction technology. This came in the form of the cable car. After enquiries in certain US and New Zealand towns where examples of the cable car system had been operating, and a close inspection of the London experience, the City Council granted a lease to the Birmingham Cable Co. which was prepared to implement a cable car system. The technology involved was fairly basic. Between the tram lines ran a narrow duct along which a steel cable moved, being continuously driven around steam-powered drums. A gripper fixed beneath the tram could be applied firmly to the cable and released again as required. In 1888 a route was established between Colmore Row and Hockley Hill, later to be extended to the New Inns, Holyhead Road, Handsworth. But the cable method posed problems. A fractured cable could bring all the trams on route to a halt. While the system was not widely extended, the Handsworth route remained operative until 1911.

The shortcomings of both cable and steam focussed attention on electricity as a possible driving power for the future. Electricity was steadily replacing steam as the power supply in manufacturing, and the Corporation was the first to sanction an experiment with a tram carrying its own power source in the form of an electric accumulator. Trials proved unsuccessful. Meanwhile, what would become a major motor omnibus company had been making commercial headway. By 1904 Birmingham Corporation decided, in effect, to take matters into its own hands and operate its own trams and buses. Overhead electric wiring appeared along steam tram routes, and 1907 brought the demise of the noisome beasts, replaced by nearly 200 trams.

By 1920/21, 631 cars had entered the fleet. Corporation motor buses were also on the increase, and for some years passengers enjoyed the choice of catching a bus or a tram along some sections of certain routes. But the maintenance, repair and replacement of tram tracks became increasingly expensive and the tramways began to lose money. In addition, the public began to show a preference for buses, with their greater flexibility of operation. Results from 1936-37 performance records show that for the first time the numbers of passengers carried by buses exceeded the total carried by trams. But for the impact of the Second World War, the Corporation would have fully implemented its policy of replacing trams with buses much earlier than 1953.

The format of this book follows closely that of Volume I. The same routes for the same year, 1937, are illustrated with different pictures. Other elements of tramways operation are also included, for example, the fares structure and the social and sporting activities of tramways personnel. In addition, a more systematic attempt has been made to depict a sample of routes withdrawn before 1937, including the Hagley Road route.

Having, at the outset, associated steam trams with Aston Villa FC, it seemed only fair to include photographs of Birmingham City and close neighbour, West Bromwich Albion. This is consistent with the emphasis placed on the tram in its social and historical contexts, literally, in fact, conveying what the 'man/woman/child in the street' might well have seen or experienced at particular moments in time.

Pass along the car please!

1

STARTING OUT

From information on the back of this card, the locomotive is a Kitson. Other firms in the same line of business included Beyer Peacock and Falcon. Almost from the outset, advertising on trams was encouraged by their owners. W.M. Taylors was an 'Exclusive Drapery Store.'

Old Square, located in Corporation Street.

The first route through Moseley to Kings Heath opened in 1887. Alcester Road formed a continuation of Moseley Road. This scene shows much of the shopping heart of 'Moseley Village'. Just left of 'Pressed Beef' can be seen a coal cart laden with full sacks of coal. Perhaps the old gentleman is telling the boy, 'Nothing like that when I was a lad!'

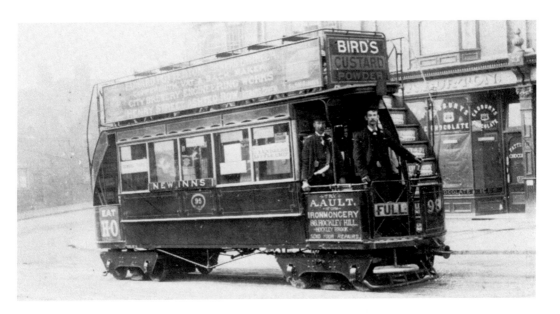

The most notable cable car route in Birmingham ran from Colmore Row. Introduced in 1888 it worked to Hockley Brook, the route being extended a year later to the New Inns, Handsworth, close to the boundary with the Black Country. Also with *In Memoriam* cards, sometimes poetic in character, the cable car said 'adieu' in 1911.

CBT Co. Ltd – shorthand for the City of Birmingham Tramways Co. Ltd, a new company formed in 1896 – received the go-ahead in 1900 from the Corporation to electrify the Bristol Road service by the overhead system. When the lease expired in 1911, CBT became part of the Corporation's fleet. CBT trams tended to be less comfortable than those of the Corporation, but were upgraded in due course.

Although this picture is rather faded, it can be seen that on car No.57 there are two smartly dressed passengers savouring the open-air 'on top'. Like driver and conductor, they are obviously interested in the photographer.

Scant regard is usually paid to the road builders without whom the safe embedding of tram lines would have been impossible. Steam rollers and their crews became a familiar sight on city streets. Presumably the scraper is designed to prevent unwanted grit, soil and tarmac building up on the roller.

2

NORTH-NORTH-WESTERN AND NORTHERN ROUTES

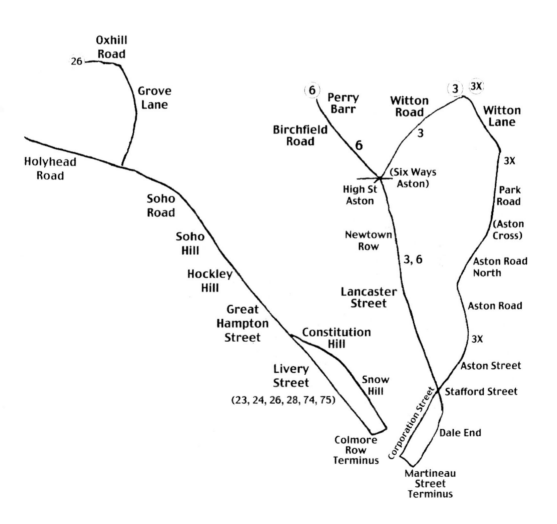

Oxhill Road

26

Grove Lane

Holyhead Road

Soho Road

Soho Hill

Hockley Hill

Great Hampton Street

Livery Street

(23, 24, 26, 28, 74, 75)

Constitution Hill

Colmore Row Terminus

6

Perry Barr

Birchfield Road

6

High St Aston

Newtown Row

Lancaster Street

Snow Hill

Corporation Street

Witton Road

3

(Six Ways Aston)

3, 6

3

3X

Witton Lane

3X

Park Road

(Aston Cross)

Aston Road North

Aston Road

3X

Aston Street

Stafford Street

Dale End

Martineau Street Terminus

The small placard on the rail of the open staircase reads 'Handsworth Depot'. A serious-looking group of uniformed drivers and conductors with, presumably, an inspector at either end stand self-consciously for the photographer. Of course, the one bloke who really has to sweat and get his hands dirty is the mechanic, complete with waistcoat, flat cap and pipe. Manly moustaches are much in vogue. The RIL is probably part of BOVRIL.

Holyhead Road started close to the West Bromwich Albion football ground, known as the Hawthorns. Running west, the road joined the Birmingham Road leading to the Black Country, a well-established tram route. To the east it joined Soho Road. The lettering on the back of the cart seems to be 'Walter Earle'. Given the sign on the standard, the four apparent workmen on the right could be waiting for a tram.

A card written on 3 August 1932. The large brick building, left, is the well-known Mitchells & Butlers New Inns, Handsworth's premier hostelry housing a banqueting room, ballroom and bowling green. The partly obscured building on the left is the Albion cinema, opened in 1916. Later it was extended to appear as shown here.

The New Inns viewed from the opposite direction at a much earlier time, the card being franked 4 September 1905. Seen here is a cable car at its suburban terminus. The road worker has paused for a moment, perhaps to pass the time of day with a passer-by.

This tram is presumably working its way to the New Inns hotel, service 28 being 'New Inns (Handsworth) and Colmore Row (rush periods only)'. The road off to the right is Booth Street. The imposing modern building on the right is the Regal cinema. Opening in 1929, this largest of suburban cinemas could seat 2,150 patrons, making a great hit on its debut with the exciting, new-fangled talkies.

Soho Road, one of the busiest thoroughfares in the city, although 'at the moment' road traffic is light. The church on the left, on the corner of Alfred Road, was opened in 1930 as the Cannon Street Memorial Church, the original church in Cannon Street, city centre, having been demolished in a road widening scheme. In the far distance a tram is just visible.

James Watt Centenary Commemoration, Birmingham, 1919.

MATTHEW BOULTON
1726–1809

JAMES WATT
1736–1819

WILLIAM MURDOCH
1754–1839

Three men who really did make a difference by helping to bring about the Industrial Revolution, and the emergence of Birmingham as the 'workshop of the world'. Their base was located in the Soho area of Handsworth, at no great distance from a number of tram stops on the Soho Road.

Heathfield Hall, the home of James Watt, was demolished *c*.1924. A reconstruction of the garret workshop was built within the Science Museum in London. In addition to devising how steam power could be used much more effectively, Watt made many other inventions including a machine for the copying of sculptures – hence the busts.

The multitude of shops on both sides of the road attracted much custom. Branches of national chain stores could be found here, including Woolworths, Peacocks, Burtons and Foster Brothers. The bank is on the corner of Baker Street, a short step from Grove Lane. There was also a homely and lively indoor market, little more than a large shed, known as the 'Rag Tag' by locals.

This building had a curious history. It opened around 1911 as an early picture house to show what were, of course, silent films. But the programme advertised seems remarkably like some of those of today, i.e. violent, sexual and generally chaotic, if far less explicit. The importance of music is evident, there being a pianist or small group of musicians to heighten the tension, the thrill of the inevitable chase, and to entertain a restive audience during intervals and mechanical breakdowns. Sadly, the cinema did not convert to talkies and was turned into a shop.

A patient tram queue forms at the corner of Nineveh Road – 'All Cars Stop Here'. The UDC building (see clock tower) also housed a public library and an art school. For a number of years Handsworth had been a residential town in Staffordshire. At the time of its absorption into Birmingham its population numbered nearly 70,000.

Situated on the corner of Stafford Road, this fine late Victorian Gothic-style building dates back to 1879, built on the site of an old inn. Its library opened in 1880. As no overhead electric wiring can be seen, these trams must be cable cars.

Having left the Council House behind and moving towards town, the tram is approaching the top of the rise before dropping down Soho Hill. Shops have given way to houses with sizeable front gardens. Amelia writes to Sue; 'How do you like this view, I was up here last night... Florence is in the Pink, she as 2 teeth.'

Following stretches of retail and residential properties, a tram heading down this hill travelled on through areas much more industrial and commercial. A building on the right, near the horse and cart, once housed the firm of Sydney Griffith, who manufactured gentlemen's 'accessories' – shirt studs and cuff links – items almost unknown today. The Jewellery Quarter is not far from this scene. Postmarked 1916.

20

In Oxhill Road, a little to the right, but out of view, the 26 service begins its journey to the city terminus in Colmore Row. This short part of the route was shared with a bus, service 11 on the Outer Circle, which, although introduced in stages, was fully operational by 1926.

The tram would take the first right-hand turn into Grove Lane 'swanking', according to some urchins, on a reserved track, but only for quite a short distance. By some postcard publishers this section was dubbed 'The Boulevard'. Soon the tram ran downhill, but still through a residential area of good-quality housing.

Handsworth   The Baths   Ana   Series 127

WESTMINSTER HANDSWORTH SWIMMING CLUB

FORTY-THIRD SEASON, 1930.

Souvenir Programme of

Championship Swimming Gala

(Under A.S.A. Laws.)

Good Evening Everybody.   Westminster-Handsworth S.C. Calling.

Price   -   SIXPENCE.

ALL RIGHTS RESERVED.

This fine municipal building stands at the corner of Grove Lane and Hinstock Road. Opened in 1907, this public facility was well patronised for many years, and not just by swimmers and would-be swimmers. It needs to be remembered that for at least the first half of the last century, very many homes had no bathroom. This, then, was the place for 'a good hot tub' when it could be afforded. At the extreme right, the railings of Handsworth Park can be seen. Postmarked 1925.

Eleven good reasons, at least for the chaps, for taking an interest in chlorinated water. Galas and competitions were common, as were regular life-saving classes and games of water polo, the latter played with vim and sometimes excess vigour. (Handsworth Swimming Club)

For many years Handsworth Park, as well as staging Scout Rallies and the like, played host to the city's annual shows (for flowers, dogs and other pets). Often included were commercial exhibits. Although the Birmingham Co–op was probably the city's largest milk supplier, Handsworth Dairies remained a major competitor. Milk was catching on as the healthy, nourishing drink of the day.

Near left, SHAVING is available, literally a cut-throat business pre-First World War. From a Handsworth address, Fred writes to pal Vic '...Pleased to receive your P.C. & that you have booked your space on a fishing smack... I suppose you had enough of the "Puffer" when you got to Penzance.' Postmarked 5 August 1913. An adventurous holiday for Vic?

Behind the tram stands Grove Lane School, on the corner of Dawson Road. This school opened in 1903, being reorganised in 1930 into an Infants and Senior Girls Department. Handsworth Grammar School for Boys, dating back to 1862 in this building, is screened by the line of trees left. Postmarked 1928.

'Anonymous' has made the right alteration. Among the shops near the two girls stood the unofficial tuck shop for Handsworth Grammar – at least during the 1930s. A dollop of ice cream in a glass of ginger pop went down a treat. Postmarked 1920s.

Grove Lane junction, left, where the 28 service ('rush periods only') joins the flow of trams in Soho Road. Nineveh Road is on the right. An intriguing advert from GUYS - Cart 15 i.e. 'Direct Supply', 'Weekly Delivery' – of what? Photograph taken in March 1939.

TRAMWAY SERVICE NUMBERS

2. Erdington and Steelhouse Lane.
35. Selly Oak and Navigation Street.
36. Cotteridge (via Pershore Road) and Navigation Street.
70. Rednal and Navigation Street.
71. Rubery and Navigation Street.
72. Longbridge and Navigation Street (occasional services only).
78. Short Heath and Steelhouse Lane.
79. Pype Hayes and Steelhouse Lane.

TROLLEYBUS SERVICE NUMBERS

92. Yardley (Church Road) and Albert Street (occasional services only).
93. Yardley (Church Road) and Station Street (rush periods only).
94. Coventry Road (City Boundary) and Albert Street.

OMNIBUS SERVICE NUMBERS
(DAYTIME SERVICES)

1. Moseley (Stratford Road) and Congreve Street.
1A. Acocks Green (via Moseley) and Congreve Street.
2B. Kings Heath and "Ivy Bush" (Hagley Road).
3A. Ridgacre Road, Harborne, and City centre.
5. Portland Road to Perry Common (via New Street, Corporation Street, Bull Street, Snow Hill and Summer Lane).
5A. Portland Road to Perry Common (Court Lane) via New Street, Corporation Street, Bull Street, Snow Hill and Summer Lane.
6. Sandon Road and City centre.
7. Perry Common to Portland Road (via Summer Lane, Snow Hill and Colmore Row)
8. Inner Circle.
9. Quinton (College Road) and City centre.
10. Quinton Road West and City centre.
11. Outer Circle.

20A

SANDON ROAD and CITY—SERVICE No. 6.

TIME TABLE—WEEK-DAYS.

Leave Sandon Road 6.45 a.m., 7.0, 7.10, 7.15, and every 3 mins. until 9.8 a.m., then 6 mins. until 5.16 p.m., then 3 mins. until 7.15 p.m., then 7 mins. until 11.12 p.m.

Leave City 7.5 a.m., 7.20, 7.25, 7.30, 7.35, and every 3 mins. until 8.48 a.m., then 6 mins. until 4.52 p.m., then 3 mins. until 7.30 p.m., then 7 mins. until 11.30 p.m.

SATURDAYS.

Leave Sandon Road as on Week-days till 12.25 p.m., then 3 mins. until 2.0 p.m., then 6 mins. till 11.12 p.m.

Leave City as on Week-days until 12.4, then 3 mins. till 2.20 p.m., then 6 mins. till 11.30 p.m.

SUNDAYS.

Leave Sandon Road 10-0, 10-20 a.m. and every 10 minutes till 11-10 p.m.
Leave City 10-20, 10-40 a.m. and every 10 minutes till 11-30 p.m.

FARES AND STAGES.

1d. Ordinary. ½d. Children's—Between

City and Granville Street	Five Ways and Rotton Park Road
Town Hall and Five Ways	Ivy Bush and Sandon Rd
Granville Street and Ivy Bush	

1½d. Ordinary. 2d. Workmen's Return. 1d. Children's—Between

City and Five Ways	Granville Street and Rotton Park Road
Town Hall and Ivy Bush	Five Ways and Sandon Road

2d. Ordinary. 3d. Workmen's Return. 1d. Children's—Between

City and Ivy Bush	Granville St and Sandon Road
Town Hall and Rotton Park Road	

2½d. Ordinary. 4d. Workmen's Return. 1d. Children's—Between

City and Rotton Park Road	Town Hall and Sandon Rd

3d. Ordinary. 4d. Workmen's Return. 1½d. Children's—Between

City and Sandon Rd

INNER CIRCLE.—Service No. 8.

TIME TABLE—WEEK-DAYS.

Leave Saltley via Aston Cross 5-45 and every 10 mins. till 6-25 a.m., 5 mins. till 7-0 a.m., then every 3¾ mins., then every 10 mins. till 12-15 p.m., then every 6 mins. till 4-40 p.m., then every 2½ mins. till 7-20, then every 5 mins. till 11-30 p.m.

Leave Saltley via Bordesley Green 5-50 and every 10 mins. till 7-0, a.m., then every 5 mins. till 7-10 a.m., then every 2½ mins. till 8-50 a.m., then every 10 mins. till 12-15 p.m., then every 6 mins. till 4-50 p.m., then 2½ mins. till 6-15 p.m., then 5 mins. till 11-30 p.m.

SATURDAYS.

Leave Saltley via Aston Cross as on Week-days till 11-45 a.m., then every 2½ mins. till 2-10 p.m., then every 5 mins. till 5-0 p.m., then every 3 mins. till 11-30 p.m.
Leave Saltley via Bordesley Green as on week-days till 11-50 a.m., then every 2½ mins. until 1-50 p.m., then every 5 mins. till 5-15 p.m., then every 3 mins. to Five Ways till 11-30 p.m.

CONTINUED ON PAGE 26a.

21A

Reference to Principal Public Buildings, &c.
shown on Aerial Map-centre of book.

	No.		No.
Art Gallery and Museum	6	Hall of Memory	2
Bingley Hall	1	King Edward's School	29
Birmingham Library	3	Market Hall	32
Blue Coat School	19	Midland Institute	10
Carrs Lane Chapel	27	Moor Street Station	28
Cathedral Church	18	New Street Station	31
Central Hall	24	Queen's College	11
Chamber of Commerce	17	Royal Society of Artists	15
Birmingham General Dispensary	21	School of Art	4
Council House	5	Smithfield Market	34
County Court	26	Snow Hill Station	30
Exchange	36	St. Martin's Church	33
Fire Brigade—Central Station	22	Technical School	13
Free Library—Central	9	Temperance Hall	16
General Post Office	14	Town Hall	8
General Post Office—Parcels Department	13	University	7
General Hospital	23	Victoria Law Courts	25

Letter Boxes on Trams and Omnibuses.
Times of Cars and 'Buses leaving the Outer Termini, and Times of Arrival at Important Loading Places and City Termini.

WEEKDAYS—

TRAMWAY ROUTES.

HALL GREEN AND DALE END. SERVICE No. 17.

From—	p.m.
Hall Green Terminus	8-44
Highfield Road	8-47
Hall Green Station	8-49
College Road	8-54
St. John's Road	8-58
Stoney Lane	9-0
Camp Hill	9-5
Dale End	9-14

REDNAL AND NAVIGATION ST. SERVICE No. 70.

From—	p.m.
Rednal Terminus	8-42
Longbridge Clock	8-45
Hawkesley Mill Lane	8-46
Bell Inn, Northfield	8-49
Selly Oak	8-53
Pebble Mill Road	9-3
Navigation Street	9-10
	9-23

RUBERY AND NAVIGATION ST. SERVICE No. 71.

From—	p.m.	From	p.m.
Rubery Terminus	8-52	Bell Inn, Northfield	9-3
Longbridge Terminus	8-55	Selly Oak	9-13
Longbridge Clock	8-56	Pebble Mill Road	9-23
Hawkesley Mill Lane	8-59	Navigation Street	9-33

OMNIBUS ROUTES.

QUINTON ROUTE. SERVICE No. 9.

From—	p.m.
Quinton Terminus	8-45
King's Head, Hagley Road	8-56
Five Ways, Edgbaston	9-3
Town Hall	9-7

BARTLEY GREEN ROUTE. SERVICE No. 12.

From—	p.m.
Bartley Green Terminus	9-5
California	9-10
Duke of York, Harborne	9-18
Five Ways, Edgbaston	9-28
Town Hall	9-32

PERRY COMMON AND PORTLAND ROAD. SERVICE Nos. 5 and 7.

From—	p.m.	From	p.m.
Perry Common Terminus	8-50	Six Ways, Aston	9-3
Ridgeway—Brookvale Rd Jct.	8-55	Town Hall	9-13
Witton Tram Terminus	9-0		

(No Saturday or Sundays Collections.)

26

A view from Birchfield Road looking towards the crossroads with Aston Lane left and Wellington Road right. A bus, service 11, can be half-seen in Aston Lane. Among the shops on the right was one dear to the heart of the cage bird fancier, selling a vast range of seeds. The drastically lopped trees stand in the beer garden of the Crown & Cushion, an Ansells house.

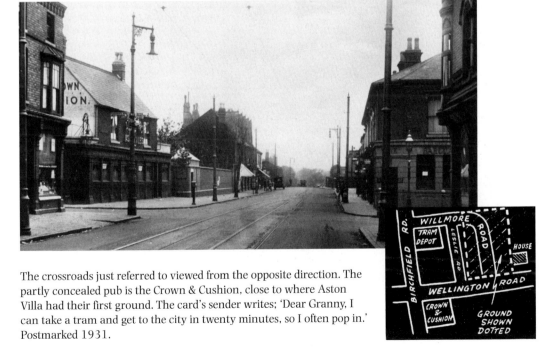

The crossroads just referred to viewed from the opposite direction. The partly concealed pub is the Crown & Cushion, close to where Aston Villa had their first ground. The card's sender writes; 'Dear Granny, I can take a tram and get to the city in twenty minutes, so I often pop in.' Postmarked 1931.

Above: A little nearer the city, with plenty of tobacco adverts on display including St Bruno, St Julien (both Ogdens brands), Players cigarettes – the ubiquitous sailor, and Turf (Phillips). Three doors away is a branch of Paynes, a firm with a good reputation for boot and shoe repairs. The small notice on the single storey building reads 'Danger Beware Of Buses', the entrance to what was once a tram depot, later shared with buses, and then housing only buses.

Left: On the back of this card is written 'Birchfield Road Garage, Perry Barr'. The slightly cocky looking chap in 'uniform' is making full use of his Brummagem gloves!

Probably a card from the late 1930s. The entrance drive to the bus garage can now be seen. Macleans was a brand of toothpaste, everywhere asking the question 'Did you Maclean your teeth today?' The building right near the corner of Bragg Road is the Birchfield Picture House, opened around 1912 and becoming very popular. Though small, it was cosy.

The Birchies, as it was known locally, is now in the background. On the corner of the Broadway, on the right, stands a typical branch of the Birmingham Municipal Bank, founded in 1919 to help and encourage 'the man in the street' to save. Nearby is what appears to be a baby Austin 7, with another one, foreground left. 'Beehive', written on the tram, was a popular city centre store.

Built in 'eastern palace style', this was the first Odeon cinema to be built in the country, opening in 1930 and situated on the corner of Birchfield and Canterbury Roads. This card was postmarked 1937. The cinema went out of commission for a spell during 1940 after an unexploded bomb needed attention following an air raid. In the early 1960s its frontage was redesigned. Later the cinema converted to a bingo club.

The 'new' frontage, hardly the stuff of 'a palace of dreams'! The low, white-faced building in Thornbury Road was a gas salesroom where household gas bills were paid.

At one time, during the period of open-top trams, and later, quite well-to-do people lived in the fine houses along this stretch of Birchfield Road between Haughton and Livingstone Roads. Fine chimneys can be glimpsed among the trees and the sturdy brick pillar gateposts and the gates themselves stand as symbols of material worth.

Beyond Heathfield Road and nearer to Six Ways Aston, gateposts, gates and chimney stacks, while still sturdy, are far less imposing than in the previous photograph. Even so, the fancy brickwork, as well as hedges and trees, catch the eye. The right-hand pavement consists of extensively used, slightly wavy-lined, deep blue bricks of great durability. Stone cobbles are also much in evidence.

One of the city's important suburban traffic hubs. Circling clockwise from the car on the left is Lozells Road, Birchfield Road, the forks of Witton Road and Victoria Road, High Street (Aston) and, by the shadow, an unseen Alma Street. Atkinsons, the rounded corner building on the right, was a well-patronised pharmacist. While not exactly inspiring, 'Take Care of Your Feet' remains sound advice.

Mr Nourse of 142 High Street, Aston, offering his customers a wide choice of newspapers and postcards. Judging from the reference to the death of W.S. Gilbert of Gilbert & Sullivan fame, the year is 1911.

In the days when cheese was cut with a wire, self-respecting grocers were uniformed in white. Here are the staff of the High Street branch of the Home & Colonial multiple grocers stores.

There is a certain grim irony about the use of 'new' in New Town Row, it being a run-down area of properties, homes and shops, overripe for redevelopment which duly came – eventually. Yes, we are still on the No.6 tram route heading in the direction of Martineau Street.

"SCOTT" SERIES, No. 1091

MITCHELLS AND BUTLERS

THE BARTONS

BIRMINGHAM THE BARTONS ARMS

This pub became one of the city's most talked about, not for its clientele or beers but for the quality and artistic merit of its fixtures and fittings. In its working heyday it was handily placed for the Aston Hippodrome (music hall) with its lively shows, the Globe Electric Palace, a 'flea-pit' cinema and the Orient cinema, close to Six Ways.

Aston Cross Picture house.

Proprietors—The Aston Cross Picture House Ltd.
Manager—H. S. Perfect.

WEEK'S PROGRAMME

Entirely British Manufacture — The City Series.

MONDAY, TUESDAY, WEDNESDAY, JUNE 25, 26, 27

1. TILLIE'S TUMBLE IN TWO REELS
Featuring Alice Howell.
Tillie leads a terrible life with her husband, who vows vengeance with a rolling pin, when Oscar, a friendly but designing neighbour, attempts to come to the rescue. Tillie shoots her spouse by mistake while trying to scare away two hungry dogs.

2. THE PURPLE DOMINO
Episode Five—" The Demon From the Sky."
Lucille and her apaches work desperately to rescue Hugo. They are successful. There is a desperate fight, and they both manage to escape.

3. THE SORROWS OF SATAN
From the world's famous novel of that title, by Marie Corelli. In Five Acts. Featuring Gladys Cooper.

TWICE NIGHTLY—Mon. & Sat. at 6-45 and 8-45
SPECIAL MATINEES—Mon. and Wed. at 3 o'clock.
Prices of Admission: Balcony 7d. (Booked for 3d extra). Floor 4d

Phone East. 430

POST CARD.

THE ADDRESS ONLY TO BE WRITTEN HERE.

Patent applied for.

THURSDAY, FRIDAY, SATURDAY, JUNE 28, 29, 30

1. Experiments in Chemistry of Combustion
(Interest)

2. SHACKLES OF BLOOD IN TWO REELS
This little domestic drama has a wonderful grip of the heart.

3. CHARLIE CHAPLIN in ONE A.M.
In TWO REELS. A scream from start to finish.

4. ON THE STEPS OF THE ALTAR
A powerful Drama. All British production.
In Four Parts.

S.P.B.

Continuous Performance, Tues. Wed. Thurs, Fri., 7 till 10-30
Children's Matinee, Sat. at 3, 1d.
Prices for Matinees, Mon. & Wed. 2½d & 5d

Book your Seats Early.

● Aston Hippodrome ●

Telephone : Aston Cross 2341
Managing Director, F. J. Butterworth   Resident Manager, James Edwardes

MAKE YOUR VISIT TO THE HIPPODROME A WEEKLY ONE
Box Office Open Daily 10 a.m. to 8 p.m.
The Tickets for seats booked by 'Phone must be claimed half-an-hour before the curtain rises.

WHY NOT BOOK YOUR SEAT PERMANENTLY ?
Doctors and other patrons expecting urgent messages may leave their seat number at the Box Office . Telephone Number for Service : Aston Cross 2341.
LIGHT REFRESHMENTS ARE AVAILABLE.

Orchestra Stalls	3/6	Dress Circle	3/-
Royal Stalls	2/9	Royal Circle	2/3
Pit Stalls	1/9	Back Circle	1/9
Boxes (Four Seats)	16/-	Balcony	1/-

6.20   Twice Nightly   8.30

Week commencing Monday, July 24th, 1950

SENSATION PRODUCTIONS, LTD., by arrangement with ANGLO-FRENCH PRODUCTIONS
present

A WOMAN DESIRED

Adapted from the French ("Femme Desiree ") by
GUSTAVE SALOU

Characters in order of appearance :

Delia Delma (a Street Walker)		EDWINA WALTON
David Lennard		FREDERICK PAYNE
Mary Saunders		HAZEL KNIGHT
" Sicilian " Joe Tabrisi (Proprietor of " The Golden Spider ")		VAN BOOLEN
" Pug " Walsh		MANVILLE TARRANT
Greta		JANET MOFFATT
Maureen	The	DAPHNE JONASON
Lilian	Golden	ELISABETH ILIFFE
Carol	Spider	MARIE SPURGEON
Norma	Girls	JOAN THOMSON
Kay		EILEEN McCARTHY
Charles Hartley		CYRIL JAMES
Denise (a Cabaret Star)		DENISE VANE
Harry Oldroyd (a Journalist)		DAVID JOHNSTON

Produced by JACK DALLAS

Synopsis of Scenes

ACT I.
Scene 1. A Street in London.
Scene 2. Backstage at " The Golden Spider " Night Club.
Scene 3. The Street.
Scene 4. " The Golden Spider."

INTERVAL

ACT II.
Scene 1. Delia's Bedroom.
Scene 2. The Street.
Scene 3. " The Golden Spider."

Manager ...   .   DAVID BANNER
Publicity Manager   ...   JACK COMBER

For SENSATION PRODUCTIONS, Ltd.

Left: The No.6 service shared its city terminus in Martineau Street with other services, including the 10 to Washwood Heath, the 8 to Alum Rock, and the 3 and 3X to Witton and Aston, the latter two services being the next to be illustrated.

Below: On certain days this industrious corner of Aston became 'aromatic' from brewing and sauce preparation, carried out by Ansells and HP respectively. The route on the left runs to Witton, and that on the right deeper into heavily industrialised Aston. An earlier cross has been replaced by the clock tower, a boundary mark of historic interest, as Aston had earlier been a manor.

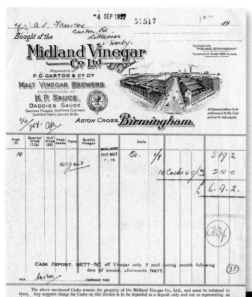

In a very neat hand a child has written: 'I thought you might like a bottle of HP sauce'. There can be much conjecture about the symbolism of the advert, but at this pre-First World War period, Britain felt pretty good about her Empire and her standing in the world.

From information on the card's back, tram 714 in Victoria Road is about to swing round into Park Road heading for Witton, presumably finishing for the day as 'Depot Only' is shown on the route sign. The traffic light appears to be at green. Has the lady on the left just bought a hat at the milliners? This photograph was taken on 29 July 1939.

For good or ill, this represents an undeniable transformation – a new Ansells brewery and a new type of constable, the white-coated traffic cop.

Given the length of Queen Victoria's reign and her high standing, more than one road in Birmingham was named after her. Six others in fact. The high building on the right, opposite the tram, housed the Aston public baths, including two swimming pools, first class and second. At weekends queues would form for the slipper baths.

Some successful swimmers from those baths. In the left-hand margin can be read 'Aston Swimming Club, Squadron Team, Champions B'ham & District 1909'. The right-hand margin reads '1st Row, S. Sizin Prof. Panting. 2nd Row P. Atkin. C. Clark. ? Leamon. H. ? Sugozy'. The term 'Prof' was commonly applied to a swimming instructor.

A road typical of Aston and many parts of the older inner suburbs. But Victoria Road lay within easy walking distance of the fine, open green space of Aston Park with its historic manor house, Aston Hall. Handy too for Villa Park, 'new' home of Aston Villa Football Club. Right, one David Lloyd advertises his involvement in the removal and storage business.

Witton Road, another of the spokes running from the hub of Six Ways, Aston, before reaching the industrial heart of Witton and its railway station. Colman's Mustard makes its mark on the corner shop close to the 'Cars Stop Here by Request' sign.

Arguably the centre of Witton, with a 3X route tram near its terminus. Behind the tram the Birmingham Co-op has moved in strength into the modern building, occupying all the shops at ground level. Photograph taken on 14 April 1938. The Typhoo Tea advert could perhaps have been worded more effectively.

And here is Witton Tram Depot as it appeared on 23 March 1939. Designed for steam trams and opened in 1882, the Aston Manor sign is an indication of the area's history. By the average traveller, Witton in general would probably be regarded, and not unfairly, as nondescript. And yet for many years it housed two of the city's major employers, staged the city's hugely popular annual fair, the Onion Fair at the Serpentine Ground, and tolerated regular invasions by football fans.

KYNOCH LIMITED.
Lion Works Witton Birmingham

Here is one of those major employers, the other being the GEC (The General Electric Co.): Kynochs (later ICI) enjoyed a worldwide reputation, principally for the working of metals, especially those of the non-ferrous kind. During two world wars the company produced massive quantities of munitions. The railway lines to the left connect Perry Barr, Witton and Aston stations.

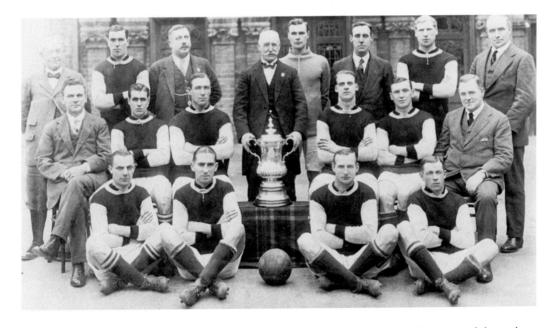

This FA cup winning team beat Huddersfield Town in the final 1-0 in extra time. Kitson scored the goal. The stars of this team included Sam Hardy (goalkeeper), Frank Moss, Andy Ducat, Billy Walker and Frank Barson, a controversial tackler.

'See you at the Holte on Saturday' – a watering hole popular with Villa fans. The terraced area at the east end of Villa Park, behind the goal, was known as the Holte End. The trams running left would be in Trinity Road adjacent to Aston Park, opposite the stadium. The right fork is Witton Lane, with the tram depot near the far end.

Something of a cornucopia of a shop. Or, to use a different image, 'packed to the gunnels' with a stock that included a great range of toys and dolls on the upper floor. For readers struggling with the lettering, this mini-store of Mr Darlington was situated on the corner of Bevington and Witton roads. This entrepreneur moved with the times – he had a telephone, East 910 Y.

Left: As a couple of passengers can be seen on the upper saloon, the tram is presumably about to start its journey. Driver and conductor certainly look ready for the day's duties. Car No.371 was one of the 301 class of trams which entered service during 1911 equipped with twenty-eight seats on top and twenty-four below. An attractive cameo of Birmingham tramways.

Below: What the public would not usually see, or hear, a confab among the tram sheds. The presence of a 'civilian' adds interest, a studious looking young man who seems to have a badge stitched to his coat. A student perhaps? Of trams? Quite probably. Thought to have been taken at Witton.

'Setting out the stall' with exuberance and abundance somewhere in Aston, next to a grocer's (see left). Given the bunches of greenery draped about, this display might form part of a sales drive just prior to Christmas. Few in Aston would be ordering turkeys, but a chicken could be within reach. The man in the white coat seems to have his order book at the ready! By his left shoulder hang the universally used brown paper carrier bags while loose newspaper pages, for wrapping, can be seen on the right.

Collecting or delivering, the Royal Mail gets through. According to the back of the card, Cyclo Gear was a company located in Potters Hill, Aston. The long jacket 'overalls' were usually known as 'cow gowns', being brown in colour.

3

NORTH-EASTERN ROUTES

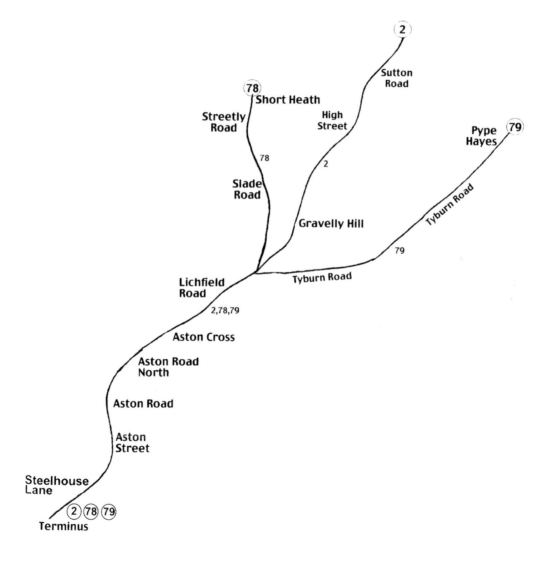

BIRMINGHAM CITY TRANSPORT

TRAMCARS

Car Nos.	Trucks		Maker and Type Motor	Year of Make
1 - 20	20	E.M.B. Bogies.	D.K. K. 30.B.	1904
21 - 70	50	Brill. 21.E.M.	D.K. 13.A.	1905/6
71 - 220	150	Brush.	G.E.C. G.E.249.	1906/7
221 - 300	80	Brill. 21.E.M.	D.K. 13.A.	1907/8
301 - 400	100	U.E.C. Single.	D.K. 13.A.	1911/12
401 - 450	50	M.&G. Single.	D.K. 13.A.	1912/13
451 - 452	2	E.M.B. Burnley Bogies.	D.K. 13.A.	1903
453 - 511	59	Mostly County.	D.K. 6.A.	Prior 1903
512 - 536	25	M.&G. Burnley Bogies.	G.E.C. W.T. 32.R.	1913/14
537 - 586	50	M.&G. Burnley Bogies.	D.K. 30 IL.	1914
587 - 631	45	Brush Burnley Bogies.	D.K. 30.IL.	1920/21
632 - 636	5	Brush Burnley Bogies.	D.K. 30.B.	1920/21
637 - 661	25	E.M.B. Burnley Bogies.	D.K. 30.B.	1923/24
662 - 701	40	E.M.B. Burnley Bogies.	D.K. 30.B.	1924/25
702 - 731	30	E.M.B. Burnley Bogies.	G.E.C. W.T. 32.H.	1925/26
732 - 761	30	E.M.B. Burnley Bogies.	D.K. 30.IL.	1926/27
762 - 811	50	E.M.B. Burnley Bogies.	D.K. 30.IL.	1928/29
812 - 841	30	M.&T. Max. Tract. Bogies.	D.K. 30.IL.	1928/29
842	1	E.E. Max. Tract. Bogie.	D.K. 105/3K.	1929
843	1	M.&T. Max. Tract. Bogie	G.E.C. W.T. 28.S.	1930

TROLLEYBUSES

'Bus Nos.	Regn. No.	Maker	Type	Date
R1 - R12		Railless Ltd.	D.D. Top covered.	1922
R13		E..B.	D.D. Top covered.	1924
R14 - R16		Railless Ltd.	D.D. Top covered.	1926
R17		A.E.C.	D.D. Top covered.	1926
R1 - R11	OV 4001 - 4011	G.E.C. Leyland.	6-Wheel.	Feb. 1927
R12 - R16	OJ 1012 - 1016	Eng.Elec.- A.E.C.	Renown.	Sept. 1932
R17 - R66	OC 1117 - 1166	G.E.C. - Leyland.	T.T.B.D.	Jan. 1934
R67 - R78	COX 67 - 78	G.E.C. - Leyland.	T.B.5.	Sept. 1937
R79 - R90	FOK 79 - 90	G.E.C. - Leyland.	T.B.7.	Feb. 1940

OLTON and CITY—Service No. 30.
TIME TABLE—WEEK-DAYS.

Leave **Olton** 6.0, 6.30 a.m. and every 10 minutes till 9.20 a.m., then 20 minutes till 5.0 p.m., then 10 minutes till 7.20 p.m., then 20 minutes till 10.40 and 10.57p.m.

Leave **Stephenson Place** 6.37, 7.7 a.m. and every 10 minutes till 8.47 a.m., then every 20 minutes till 4.57 p.m., then 10 minutes till 7.57 p.m., and then 20 minutes till 10.57 p.m. and 11.15 and 11.30 p.m.

SATURDAYS.

Leave **Olton** 6.0 a.m., 6.30 a.m., and every 10 mins. till 9.20 a.m., every 20 mins. till 12.0 noon, every 10 mins. till 2.0 p.m., every 20 mins. till 5.20 p.m., every 10 mins. till 10.55 p.m.

Leave **Stephenson Place** 6.34 a.m., 7.7 a.m., and every 10 mins. till 9.57 a.m., every 20 mins. till 12.37 p.m., every 10 mins. till 2.17 p.m., every 20 mins. till 5.57 p.m., every 10 mins. till 11.30 p.m.

SUNDAYS.

Leave **Olton** (Warwick Road) 9.40 a.m. and every 20 minutes until 10 p.m., 10.22 p.m., 10.52 p.m.

Leave **Stephenson Place** 10.14 a.m., and every 20 minutes until 10.34 p.m., 10.56 p.m., 11.26 p.m.

These Buses traverse the City Centre via New Street, Colmore Row. Bull Street and Corporation Street.

FARES AND STAGES

1d. ORDINARY.   ½d. CHILDREN'S—BETWEEN.

Avondale Road and Russell Road	Russell Road and Shirley Road
Shaftmoor Lane (Stratford Road Junction) and Fox Hollies Road	Fox Hollies Road and Olton Terminus

1½d. ORDINARY.   2d. RETURN.   1d. CHILDREN'S—BETWEEN

Stoney Lane and Russell Road	Shaftmoor Lane (Stratford Road Junction) and Shirley Road
Avondale Road and Fox Hollies Road	Russell Road and Olton Terminus

2d. ORDINARY.   3d. RETURN.   1d. CHILDREN'S—BETWEEN

Stratford Place and Russell Road	Shaftmoor Lane (Stratford Road Junction) and Olton Terminus
Stoney Lane and Fox Hollies Road	
Avondale Road and Shirley Road	

2½d. ORDINARY.   4d. RETURN.   1d. CHILDREN'S—BETWEEN

Alcester Street and Russell Road	Stoney Lane and Shirley Road
Stratford Place and Fox Hollies Road	St. John's Road and Olton Terminus

3d. ORDINARY.   4d. RETURN.   1½d. CHILDREN'S—BETWEEN

Station Street and Russell Road	Stratford Place and Shirley Road
Alcester Street and Fox Hollies Road	Stoney Lane and Olton Terminus

3½d. ORDINARY.   5d. RETURN.   1½d. CHILDREN'S—BETWEEN

City and Russell Road	Alcester Street and Shirley Road
Station Street and Fox Hollies Road	Stratford Place and Olton Terminus

4d. ORDINARY.   6d. RETURN.   2d. CHILDREN'S—BETWEEN

City and Fox Hollies Road	Station Street and Olton Terminus

4½d. ORDINARY.   6d. RETURN.   2d. CHILDREN'S—BETWEEN
City and Olton Terminus.

Only Tickets to Russell Road and beyond will be issued on Buses from City

FARES AND STAGES TO CITY ONLY,

1d. ORDINARY.   ½d. CHILDREN'S

Shaftmoor Lane (Stratford Road Junction) to Stoney Lane	Stoney Lane to Alcester Street
St. John's Road to Stratford Place	Stratford Place to Station Street
	Alcester Street to City

1½d. ORDINARY.   2d. RETURN.   1d. CHILDREN'S

Shaftmoor Lane (Stratford Road Junction) to Stratford Place	Stoney Lane to Station Street
St. John's Road to Alcester Street	Stratford Place to City

2d. ORDINARY.   3d. RETURN.   1d. CHILDREN'S

Shaftmoor Lane (Stratford Road Junction) to Alcester Street	St. John's Road to Station Street
	Stoney Lane to City

2½d. ORDINARY.   4d. RETURN.   1d. CHILDREN'S

Shaftmoor Lane (Stratford Road Junction) to Station Street	St. John's Road to City

3d. ORDINARY.   4d. RETURN.   1½d. CHILDREN'S
Shaftmoor Lane (Stratford Road Junction) to City

SPECIAL NOTICE.

This Guide is the only Publication that contains all the present "declared Highways" within the City Boundary, numbering more than 300 New Roads, Avenues, Groves, Crescents, etc., constructed in connection with the numerous City Housing Estates—Municipal and Private.

A list of the Estates is also given on back of Map, and how they are reached by Tram or 'Bus from the City Centre, and vice versa.

N.B.—For Advertising Rates apply to—

THE TRAM GUIDES Co.,
COUNTY BUILDINGS,
147, CORPORATION STREET,
BIRMINGHAM.

Telephone—Central 7895.

CROSS CITY 1d. FARES.

Passengers may now ride between Snow Hill and Station Street on Omnibus Services Nos. 13, 13a, 15, 15a, 16, 29 and 30 and between General Hospital and Station Street on Omnibus Service No. 17 for One Penny.

Postmarked 1947, when Britain was still painfully recovering from the Second World War. While many goods were still rationed, this company seems to be making a good fist of living up to its name and implying that the future lies with cars. Left is a 'Ruby' Austin, a model introduced in the mid-1930s, an immensely popular small car. More stock is on show upstairs. Premier Motor Co. Aston Road.

The work of these two tram services is nearly done, the photograph having been taken in 1951. All routes were closed down by August 1953. There is a certain irony about the 'Aladdin's Cave' of a builders merchants for, at this time, building materials remained in desperately short supply.

Left: Aston Cross and a closer look at the clock tower that, in 1891, replaced an earlier boundary mark. To the left is the start of Lichfield Road, following on from Aston Road.

Below: Aston formed a densely populated, highly industrialised suburb and a tram journey through it, including Lichfield Road, would amply confirm that description. Among the many shops was this one, catering for the needs of the gardener, nurseryman, poultry keeper (a few chickens in the backyard), allotment holder, dog owner, pet owner and cage bird fancier.

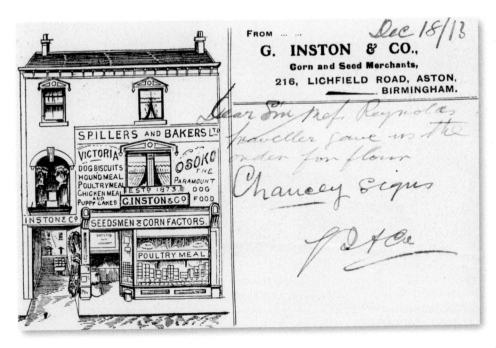

The outlook improves, a photograph taken in May 1947 of a cross-city service, the No.5 from Lozells to Slade Road via Gravelly Hill. Car No.526 dates back to 1913/14, its open balconies on top becoming enclosed during the late 1920s.

Photographed in 1923, the note on the back of this card reads 'Aston Road linking to Salford Bridge, New Double Roadway & Central Tramway Reservation under Construction' – an appropriate undertaking, but only some 600 yards in length. The camera is looking towards Salford Bridge which spanned a river and canal.

Above: A dual carriageway, but a scaled down version of a reservation, the bridge width probably imposing limitations. The tram is on the 79 route from Pype Hayes to Steelhouse Lane. Today, high overhead, the most complicated of motorway 'roundabouts', Spaghetti Junction, soars and roars above this erstwhile relatively calm scene.

Left: It is thought that for a time this missionary caravan was stationed somewhere near Salford Bridge. The Church Army owes its origins (1880s) to the zeal and enterprise of a young Anglican curate, William Carlisle (1847–1942). His army was accommodated within the broader church. The uniform is by no means martial.

Moving through the tangle of Salford Bridge tram junction, the left-hand tram is heading for Slade Road. The No. 2 is preparing to tackle the steadily rising Gravelly Hill, while the track forking right is for the 79 service from Tyburn Road to Pype Hayes. The traffic policeman on his tiny island appears to be helping someone to find his way. This scene was photographed in July 1939.

A view photographed in July 1953, the month of the last tram rides and rites. The No. 2 is heading up Gravelly Hill and the 78 is leaving Slade Road. Before long (1959) Atkinsons of Aston Ales will have been taken over by Mitchells & Butlers. On its signboard the Atkinson 'trademark' can just be made out: an elderly, jovial man holding out a pint, admiring the colour and the clarity of the beer in his glass.

A rather pleasant residential road with enough going on – shopping, delivering, travelling – to enliven the scene. The unattended bicycles are more likely than not without security locks and chains.

More detail can now be seen about Slade Road shops. The laundry needs little by way of display in its window. The stationer next door selling Rajah Cigars has a fully stocked window. A blind shelters the wares of a High Class Meat Purveyor, while the jumble on the pavement suggests that a greengrocer is a neighbour. A pony and trap wait across the way. The way people are dressed indicates that this is a pre-First World War photograph.

At 341 Slade Road stands an enterprising bakery offering a delivery service to the customer's door. This practice, at least for the Birmingham Co-op and others, lasted into the 1950s. At first floor level, left of HOVIS, can be seen Wills Gold Flake, a popular, slightly 'better' brand of cigarettes.

An early terminus for an early tram route at the far end of Slade Road. Car No.223 began work in 1907 and the clothing of the children, for whom the tram was probably an exciting novelty, is certainly pre-First World War.

In 1926 the No.2 route was extended from Stockland Green to Short Heath, along a mile of reserved track lined with trees. The Plaza cinema was opened in 1927 on what was a triangular site. After the cinema's closure in 1978, the building was converted into a bingo hall and later a supermarket.

Nearing the end in time and space: 9 May 1953, near the terminus at Short Heath of the 78 service from Steelhouse Lane. This is a fine example of a central reservation, flanked either side by broad roads, as yet uncongested.

On the right, Kingsbury Road branches away in the direction of Chester Road. As the walls, gates and trees show, this is a pleasant residential area. The church on the corner is a Methodist chapel (Free United). Opposite the chapel stood a very large house in spacious grounds, Gravelly Hill House. The hill was so-called from the various gravel pits once worked in the area.

Six Ways, Erdington. Yet another hub, this time with the spokes of Gravelly Hill North, Reservoir Road, Summer Road, Sutton New Road, High Street and Wood End Road. The No.2 tram service travelled along High Street. The signposts display a variety of destinations and mileages. 'Archers Supply Stores' feature on many postcards, as does that 'blooming roundabout', thought to be one of the first built in the country to regulate traffic.

Part of the High Street was narrower than shown here, necessitating a single-tram track for part of its length. As was often the way with roads that had once constituted village high streets, this one in Erdington remained a popular shopping area. It also contained a small cinema, the Erdington Picture House, opened in 1913.

The single-line track mentioned above, photographed on 21 September 1938. The '64' refers to the 'turnback' status of the tram. Baines, left, had a chain of bakers' shops. Motor traffic is on the increase, Belisha pedestrian crossings are becoming more accepted and the general awareness of the need for improved road safety is rising.

TRAM TERMINUS ERDINGTON.

Banks seemed to like having some of their branches on prominent street corners. This particular branch is part of the Midland Bank. Before the No.2 route was extended to a terminus near the city boundary with Sutton Coldfield, this was its terminus, rather an unusual site between the road and the line of shops.

Sutton New Road, Erdington.

Eventually, in 1938, High Street was by-passed by enlarging Sutton New Road and creating a central reservation. The new two-storey building is for the GPO, presumably fit for purpose if not particularly pleasing to the eye.

'Last car on Saturday night High Street Erdington', is the cryptic note written on this card. A snapshot from 24 September 1938. Given the signs on the right, could the tram be outside a dance hall, a cinema, the Erdington Picture House? Dancing, 'Saturday night hops' at all kinds of venues, and picture-going were both highly popular in 1938. According to the 1937 timetable, the last tram left Erdington at 11.02 p.m.

Initially starting at Gravelly Hill, the Tyburn Road was built to facilitate access to the massive Dunlop factory. For the same reason, the tram track was laid to help employees travel to work. Photograph taken in June 1953.

Founded by John Boyd Dunlop (1840–1921), Dunlop, trailblazing pneumatic tyres, soon required and built a larger factory in rural Erdington, opening in 1917 close to Tyburn Road. Dunlop went on to further success with their production of cycle saddles, tool bags, plimsolls and tennis balls. The firm achieved worldwide custom for their vehicle tyres.

LORD BURGHLEY

Some major Birmingham employers provided recreational facilities for their employees with sports grounds at a distance or close by, as with Cadbury. Birmingham's Gas Department had a sports ground in Erdington, where on 15 June 1929 the Midland Counties athletic championships were held. Seen here is Lord Burghley, a prominent athlete, being presented with a medal by his wife.

4

EASTERN ROUTES

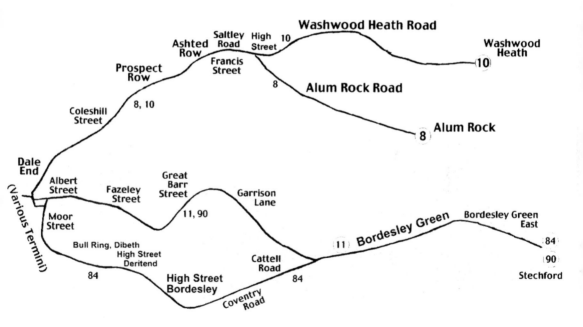

Very much an inner suburb, reached by the 8 and 10 tram services from Martineau Street, Saltley was 'famous' for, among other things, a teachers' training college and a massive gas works. As can be seen, its High Street was like many another. The atmosphere seems murky and industrial, but with shop blinds out, the sun and warmth cannot be far away. The uniformed messenger boy (telegram deliverer) appears keen to be photographed.

Trams were probably held up for quite a time as this horse-drawn 'wagon train' got under way. Given the amount of public interest shown in High Street, Saltley, for this army convoy, it could be that the First World War is imminent or in its early stages when optimism about an early victory ran high.

The card's sender writes, 'I live quite near to this road and I travel up & down it daily I must say I do not think over much of it'. Be that as it may, this is self-evidently a busy shopping centre, pre-First World War, given what people are wearing.

A little further on in time and space. Unfortunately the newspaper placards cannot be read, except in one case, left of the shop's door, where even casual observers might be intrigued by 'His Lucky Trail'. Cadbury's Chocolate can be read above the doorway. Postmarked 1919.

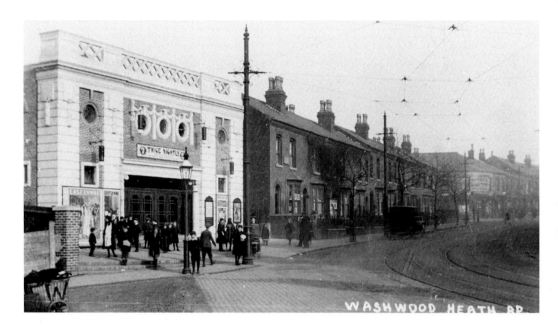

Given the youngsters' clothing, these are the early days of the cinema, showing silent films. Almost certainly this picture house is the Grand, Alum Rock, opened before the First World War. The film being shown, *East Lynne*, if based on the immensely popular novel of the same title by Mrs Henry Wood, will be a real tear-jerker. Plenty of sentimental music ('orchestral music' – beneath title) available.

Heading for leafier suburbs. This is a long road, but at about the halfway point on the southern edge stretched Ward End Park. On the back of the horse-drawn van can be read 'No 472 Brooke Bond Tea'.

Perhaps appropriate weather has arrived for what is described on the card's back as, 'Sept 50 last day of operation' for service 10 'Washwood Heath (Fox and Goose) and Martineau Street'. The cinema is the Beaufort, Coleshill Road, Ward End, which opened in 1929, being enlarged in 1937 to seat 1,500 people.

Perhaps a fair number of local cinema fans worked at this factory, the Midland Railway Carriage Co., or at Wolseley motor works next door, on the northern side of Washwood Heath Road. The factory shown began work in 1912, being purposely designed for the manufacture and repair of wooden-bodied railway wagons. This company had a long history of wagon building dating back to the middle of the nineteenth century.

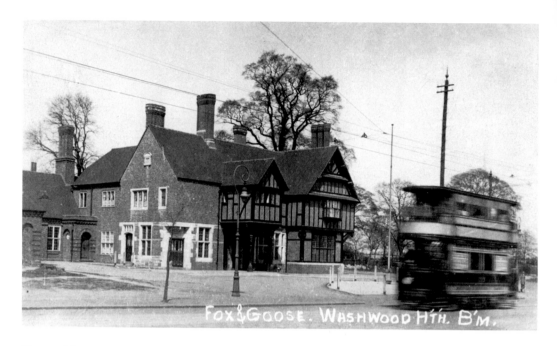

FOX&GOOSE. WASHWOOD HTH. B'M.

This card features one of those handy tram termini imaginatively situated by a well-known, spacious pub, a rebuilt version of an earlier inn which had stabled horses. In this photograph there is some parking space for motor cars. Postmarked 1919.

A view from a different corner revealing yet another sizeable traffic roundabout, sure to arouse heated comment! At this junction Washwood Heath Road crosses into Coleshill Road. A bollard, right, stands in Bromford Lane which crosses into Stechford Lane. Just below the semi-circular window across the way this lettering can be made out: 'Coleshill Road Post Office'.

Service 12, shown here, had stopped running by 1937, but the 84 and 90 came together in Bordesley Green to continue to Stechford. By both trams little knots of people indicate that getting on and getting off are under way. Note the distance, left, from the pavement to the tram, a traffic hazard of which passengers were well aware. 'Ruby' refers only to lighting a gas ring and the like, and not a dating agency!

The two key public service stations, police and fire, are sandwiched between Fordrough Lane and Humpage Road, a cul-de-sac. The opening on the right leads to Imperial Road. At some distance, the home of the sender of the card is approximately marked, with an X. A Cadbury advert can be seen, as can that bearded sailor of Players.

W.A. Camwell, a noted photographer of trams, writes: 'Bordesley Green turnback – one-time terminus looking towards Stechford 24/9/38'. At the corner shop a familiar advert can be seen. No coyness on the part of Beechams! The tram driver has probably just clocked in at the Bundy clock, a key time control of the tramway system.

The note on the back of the card states 'Start of Reserved Track Bordesley Green East'. Another view of Car No.843, the last new tram in the city, which entered service in 1930. A lightweight, but in one sense only, its body being constructed of aluminium.

Stechford Railway Station was no great distance from the tram terminus. This attractively designed, well-built group of shops and living accommodation are pleasing to the eye, as are the virtually uniform lace curtains, usually a signal of respectability. The names of three shopkeepers appear to be Glover, Emberton and Baldwin, the last named being a hardware store, while Glover was a newsagent/tobacconist. A better class of cigarette is advertised here, Lambert & Butlers.

Stechford tram terminus on 18 April 1948. Cars 843 (again), 358, 373, 357 and 382 awaiting the 'off'. *Everybody's* was a weekly news, comment and lavishly illustrated magazine.

Another reminder that road builders and repairers are indispensable to any road traffic system. A scribbled note on the card's back reads 'Birmingham Jan 1911 Concreters'. Concrete road sections were relatively new at this time, but solid rubber tyres on the increasing numbers of vehicles were damaging tarmacked surfaces. This carefully posed photograph well portrays the navvies' virtual uniform. Not a bare head to be seen. A classic illustration of how labour intensive some types of work still were.

But mechanisation was steadily on the increase. Although the scribble on the back is hard to decipher, there is a clear reference to Stratford Road, Birmingham, being the location.

5

SOUTHERN AND SOUTH-WESTERN ROUTES

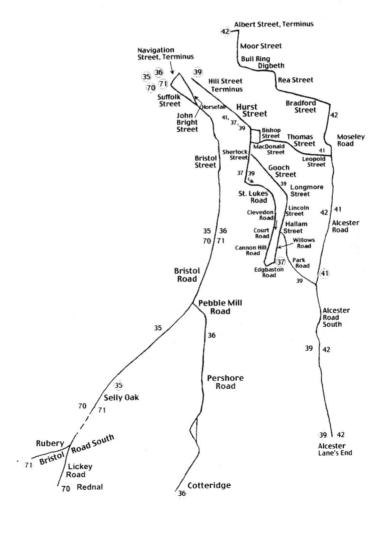

Albert Street, Terminus
42
Moor Street
Navigation
Street, Terminus
Bull Ring
Digbeth
35 36
39
Rea Street
70 71
Hill Street
Terminus
Suffolk
Street
Horsefair
Hurst
Street
Bradford
Street
42
John
Bright
Street
41, 37, 39
Bishop
Street
Thomas
Street
Moseley
Road
Sherlock
Street
MacDonald
Street
41
Bristol
Street
37 39
Gooch
Street
Leopold
Street
St. Lukes
Road
39
Longmore
Street
Clevedon
Road
Lincoln
Street
42 41
Court
Road
Hallam
Street
Alcester
Road
35 36
70 71
Cannon Hill
Road
Willows
Road
37
Park
Road
Edgbaston
Road
39
41
Bristol
Road
Alcester
Road
South
Pebble Mill
Road
35
36
39 42
Pershore
Road
35
Selly Oak
70 71
Rubery
Bristol Road South
71
Lickey
Road
70 Rednal
39 42
Alcester
Lane's End
Cotteridge
36

The 42 service tram stands at its city centre terminus in Albert Street, near Dale End. The suburban destination, via Moseley Road, is Alcester Lane's End. The tram's top vestibules are still well ventilated in 1949. Car No.436 was one of a batch of fifty that entered service during 1912/13.

This is the Rea Street–Bradford Street junction. The street name plates can just be made out on the walls. A sizeable warehouse for tyres, including Pirellis, occupies the corner, and some serious roadworks are under way, given the size of the arched shelter. Or maybe telephone repairs?

A scene from an earlier time when a tram service, No.40, ran to Kings Heath along the 42 route, passing through Balsall Heath on the way.

The boy's knickerbockers and a half-penny stamped card provide good clues, this scene pre-dating 1914. Behind the tree can be seen 'Camp Hill Station', a railway station.

A 41 service car turning from Moseley Road into, well, the writing is literally on the wall of 'Hands Expert Tailor'. Some entrepreneur from High Street, Kings Heath, is advertising his wares on the front of the tram. There is also a choice of drinks – tea and whisky. Note the knee-length clothes – just below if older – for the ladies of 1949.

This scene is at the southern end of the journey, with the tram heading for town. Again there are indications that this photograph dates from the early years of the twentieth century. The tram has a two digit number which signifies that it entered service no later than 1907. 'Crawfords' was usually followed by 'cream crackers', and that seems to be the case here!

A photograph from June 1948 revealing the sylvan junction of Park Road and Alcester Road, from which point services 39 and 42 worked the same route to Alcester Lanes End. The bus, if it is a 17, has much further to go, its route running from Maypole Lane, south of the tram terminus, via the city centre to Chester Road, Erdington, on the city's northern perimeter.

Another fine Camwell photograph of trams at the Hill Street city terminus in 1949. In 1937 the 37 route had started in Navigation Street, finishing at Cannon Hill. 'Tizer' was a popular sparkling soft drink bearing the slogan 'Tizer the appetiser'. Showing at the West End cinema is *Walter Mitty*, starring Danny Kaye. To this day the term Walter Mitty is applied to an alleged fantasist.

The road that is 'missing' is Willow Road, the location of the tram. From this 'traffic control', meaning the island, Cannon Hill Park and the Warwickshire County Cricket Club ground are little more than a good cricket ball throw away.

Handsworth Park and Cannon Hill Park vied for the status of the city's most prestigious park. Cannon Hill was created from an estate given to the city in 1873 by Miss Louisa Anne Ryland, a notable philanthropist. Here we have a tranquilly happy scene from between the wars. A fisherman is present, if not immediately apparent.

Two of the city's longest and most direct tram routes started from Navigation Street, these being the 70 to Rednal and the 71 to Rubery. Their route was shared nearly all the way. The first part, from the city, went along Bristol Street, which soon became Bristol Road.

An early scene, this card carries an intriguing message. Lizzie writes to Amy in Jersey: 'We had a lovely time on Wednesday at the Mayor's garden party, the gardens were lovely – heaps of people I knew...' Sounds like a budding socialite! Fine properties are now beginning to appear on each side of this Edgbaston road. This card was posted in Kidderminster in 1907.

This scene is typical of the long stretch of gracious, older properties, a sort of well-heeled ribbon development with splendid houses carefully screened from view. In earlier times, in different parts of the city, some objections to proposed tram routes had been made on the grounds that passengers 'on top' would be able to peer into private front gardens.

The spanking new red-brick university in Bournbrook, opened by King Edward VII and Queen Alexandra in 1909, is visible from passing trams. The clock tower was affectionately known by generations of students as 'Joe', in recognition of the sterling work carried out by Joseph Chamberlain to improve the city in a number of significant ways.

An erstwhile small community close to an actual Bourn Brook. Who has not heard of Bournville, also nearby?

Here is a Bournbrook shop worthy of admiration. Mr Wake is certainly alive to the notion, 'if you've got it, flaunt it!' Some artistic thought has gone into his display. Consider the symmetry of the tin baths, coal scuttles and buckets. The sentry box of trellis is packed with protective materials. Prizes are being offered to help a Day Adult School, Selly Oak (the books are in the background). Two washing dollies can be seen on the left, and right, and Venetian Red and Yellow Ochre are for sale.

16040 SELLY OAK INSTITUTE.

Selly Oak is so named because of the venerable oak tree that once grew very close to the main road. Although it caused some local unhappiness, the tree eventually had to be cleared away. This card, conveying Christmas greetings, was written in 1909. The coat of arms is, of course, that of Birmingham, the figures representing industry and art, with 'Forward' as the motto.

SELLY OAK HOSPITAL

This hospital developed out of an earlier infirmary and became a major hospital of South Birmingham. It stands but a short distance from tram stops on the Bristol Road. The Outer Circle bus, No.11, works along Oak Tree Lane and passes the hospital's entrance. The message on the card includes 'beautiful grounds, have not been round them yet' – perhaps the first impressions of a new hospital employee.

BRISTOL RD & THE OLD SCHOOLS - SELLY OAK.

A view looking towards town with the tram route moving away from the crossroads of Harborne Lane, left, and Oak Tree Lane, right. Among the shops is a branch of the well-known grocers, Wrensons.

GRIFFINS HILL SELLY OAK.

After the short rise out of Selly Oak, the dual carriageway drops down this hill, passing Woodbrooke College on the left, before reaching Bournville Lane with its green and pleasant areas both sides of the road, the Cadbury family having played an important part in this achievement.

The dual carriageway and central reservation began just out of Selly Oak. Whitehill Lane runs left of the tram, leading to an area where many new houses were built on Bournville Village Trust land during the 1950s and '60s. Opposite stands 'The Woodlands', once the home of George Cadbury who gifted the house for use as a convalescent home for crippled children, the home being opened in 1909. After various developments, it became an orthopaedic hospital.

Before being absorbed into Birmingham in 1911, Northfield had been a country village. Its character began to change as large, modern factories established themselves nearby, Cadbury, Kalamazoo and at Longbridge, of course, the Austin Motor Co. To the left, Bell Hill drops steeply to Merritts Brook. The Bell Hotel was a Davenports house, a brewery that at one time delivered to the householder's doorstep. The shop beneath the clock is Huins, a quality shoe shop.

Bristol Road South, Northfield.

This is nearing journey's end, whether Rednal or Rubery. On the track city cobbles have been replaced by stone ballast. It is possible that among the trees on the right stretches the factory of Kalamazoo. At one time some 500 workers were employed by the claimed 'principal loose leaf manufacturers in Europe'.

The gateway to the Lickey Hills, an extensive area of unspoiled countryside where five-and-a-half-day-working-week Brummies and their families could virtually roam at will, play games, have a picnic, meet up with friends at the Bilberry tea rooms, then happily queue up for the tram home. Usually the busiest pleasure day of the year was August Bank Holiday Monday.

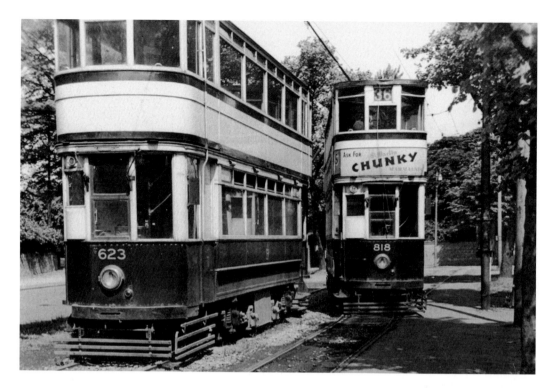

This is an example of a single line working in Pebble Mill Road by the 36 service, from Navigation Street to Cotteridge. Having travelled along Bristol Road from the city, near Edgbaston Park, the tram turned left into Pebble Mill and then right into Pershore Road.

A pleasant run brought the tram to Ten Acres, an area of some independent and enterprising spirit, given that joining forces with Stirchley, a separate Co-op organisation, was established. This was known as TASCOS – Ten Acres & Stirchley Co-op Society. Being founded in 1875, this pre-dated the Birmingham Co-op. Some Cadbury workers would use the tram to alight in Stirchley, the factory being just a short walk away up Bournville Lane.

A Cotteridge tram terminus awaiting customers on a wet day. There is not even a window shopper about, even though some of the shops seem to have interesting stock, for instance 'Picture Frames and Art Depot'. But the card's message stirs the imagination: 'I shall be very much obliged if you would send me a Bottle for a Ball Friday night it is the last of the season.' Presumably, the bottle was to contain scent. Postmarked 1908.

Little or no fragrance to be found here, in 1952, in the yard of the Cotteridge Tram Depot!

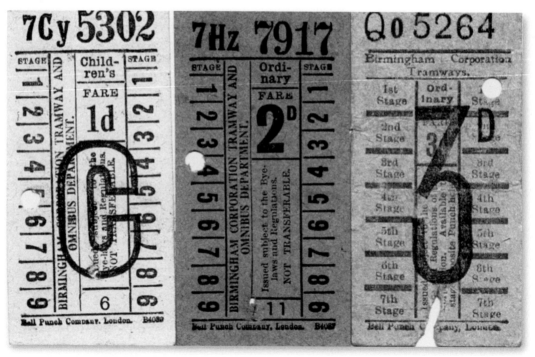

6

WESTERN AND NORTH-WESTERN ROUTES

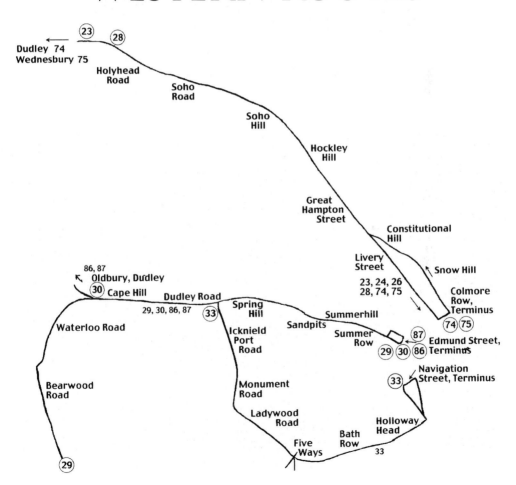

From Navigation Street terminus, the 33 service worked to Holloway Head, then Bath Row, the location of this hospital. Founded in 1840, later called Queens and further developed, this is how the hospital appeared in the late 1920s. Once a new hospital, the Queen Elizabeth in Edgbaston opened in 1938, the Queens eventually became a highly renowned Accident and Rehabilitation Centre.

ISLINGTON ROW. (1) BIRMINGHAM.

From Bath Row the trams moved into Islington Row. This card was used to send birthday greetings to 'Dear Dad', away in the Isle of Man. The nearer tram is moving towards Five Ways, Edgbaston.

And here is Five Ways, Edgbaston, a much photographed location. Again, because of a nosey boy in knickerbockers and white collar, this is probably a pre-First World War snapshot. From the start of Hagley Road we are looking across to Broad Street. The statue is of Joseph Sturge (1794–1859), a Birmingham industrialist and reformer. Seemingly, ice is being delivered, right, presumably to FIVE WAYS FISH HA (see above), at just turned eight o'clock, surely in the morning.

The 29 service started in Edmund Street, running to Bearwood. 'From city all cars stop here', states the sign on the standard. The location is Dudley Road, and in the background can be seen part of Dudley Road Hospital which has a long and complicated history. The adverts, 1929, speak for themselves.

Cape Hill was the home of Mitchells & Butlers vast brewery, known for its leaping deer trademark. It was in 1898 that Mitchell joined forces with Butler. The Waterloo was an imposing house at the junction of five roads of which Cape Hill was one. On the card's back, beside an illegible signature, is written, 'September 25th 1913.'

This provides a good overview of a corner of Staffordshire. No white helmet here for traffic control. On the right stands a branch of Marsh & Baxter's, multiple pork butchers well known for their sausages and their adverts. At first floor level a pig can be seen harnessed to a small four-wheeled cart laden with sausages. As a boy, in harsher times, the author found this caption highly amusing: 'drawing his own conclusion'.

This van is likely to be one of a fleet, presumably for the delivery of crated bottles. While equipped with modern pneumatic tyres, the lamps near the windscreen could be of the acetylene type.

Waterloo Road and Bearwood Road linked Cape Hill and Hagley Road West, near to the Kings Head Inn. By the bank heads are bowed, which could be due to all manner of causes, but it is worth remembering that at the time the card was posted (1917) the country was enduring the third year of war and suffering enormous loss of life on the Western Front.

This is the Bearwood terminus for the 29 service where the regulation Bundy clock stands to attention. Another branch of Wrensons is close by. This photograph was taken on 30 August 1938, when war seemed imminent but another year of uneasy peace was to prevail.

A little girl, Doris, writes: 'we are spending our holiday at Smethwick and this is a view of a street close to us...' – probably a holiday with relatives, Smethwick not being a known holiday resort! The tram may not be a Birmingham car, but the city's 86 service did work Edmund Street to Oldbury. Of interest is the slightly grisly advert, but more people than previously could now afford artificial teeth. This card was posted in 1911.

'No dogs allowed inside the car', states the rule below the conductor's arm, and above it, 'Passengers entering or leaving the car while in motion do so at their own risk'. The signboard appears to read: 'Birmingham W'Mill Lane [Windmill Lane] Smethwick, Spon Lane and Oldbury'. Greys, in Bull Street, Birmingham, was the city's top store until challenged by Lewis's.

Three coalmen pause and pose for a fag break, probably well earned. Hundredweight sacks full of coal carried on the back and humped along narrow pathway entries to domestic coalhouses was hard graft. Household open fires lasted well into the 1960s. Delivery work of this kind was widespread, but the above lorry hails from Old Hill in the Black Country. 'Coal fires for Health...' – well, we know better now, but if the last and hidden word is 'Warmth' then that is certainly accurate.

On match days trams from both directions were vital to many West Bromwich Albion football fans. The ground, called the Hawthorns, while in West Bromwich lay only a few yards from the Birmingham boundary at Handsworth. This scrambling aboard scene is from 1938 and may be for reasons other than a football match, but 'Hawthorns' is scribbled on the back of the card.

Sadly there is no silverware on display. 'West Brom' was a club with a relatively long history, having been one of the founder members of the First Division in 1888/89. Often referred to as 'The Baggies', held to be a comment at one time on the spacious long shorts worn by the players. (Team of 1913–1914)

From Colmore Row in the city to Wednesbury in the Black Country was the 75 run, shown here in March 1939, with the car travelling west away from the Hawthorns. On this flat, straight stretch the driver could notch up speeds noticeably above the average.

West Bromwich High Street, another busy shopping street, as the 87 makes its way to Carter's Green, then on to Dudley, having started in Edmund Street. 'Target' adverts appear to be followed by 'Clothing Stores for Value.' Next door, right, we are informed that 'Seal Jackets and Furs Cleaned, Dyed and Altered.' At this time, possibly 1915, such a commercial activity would not have been in the least controversial.

A few days before Britain declared war against Germany on 3 September 1939, W.A. Camwell took this photograph of this entrance to Dudley, looking towards Birmingham. Out of sight but close by lie the ruins of Dudley Castle and the splendid new zoo, spacious and of advanced design.

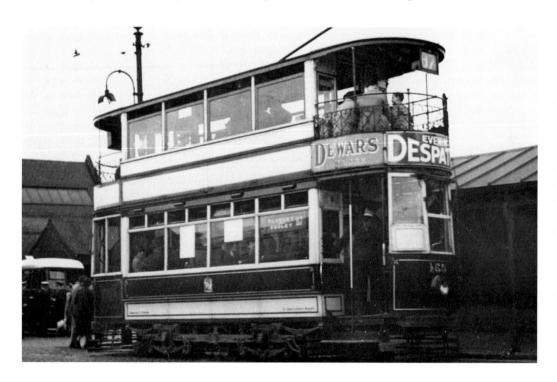

On the back of this photograph another tram buff has written: 'Car 159 at Dudley Terminus. This route was closed on 30/9/39.' Being numbered 159, this car must have experienced much wear and tear, and repair, having entered service during 1906/07, spending over thirty years in the business!

7

TWO 'CROSS-CITY' ROUTES

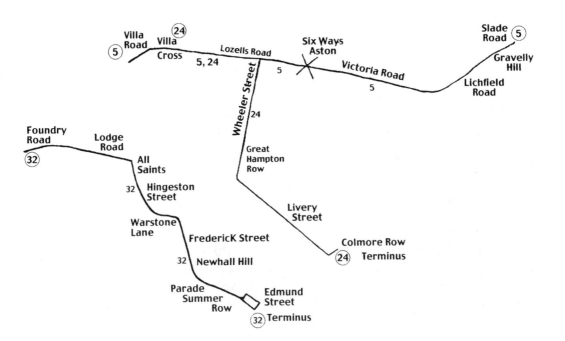

A view taken almost from the suburban terminus of service 5, Lozells to Slade Road and Gravelly Hill. In the distance a faintly coloured old pub can just be seen, the Villa Cross. The rather showy, half-timbered shop on the corner of Hamstead Road became widely known as 'Bendalls' Corner' after the two sisters who ran this bakery/confectioners.

This card carries a message in good French, written by an English girl to 'une amie – Merci bien pour PC', dated 7 August 1918. The shopping thoroughfare containing fine late Victorian properties was popular with residents from Handsworth and Lozells. 'Franklin & Poole' can be read as being 'Family Drapers'. Above the horse-drawn cart can be read 'Finch Road Bakers'. A short distance away could be found Baines Model Bakery which issued many sets of self-promotional postcards.

A photograph taken from the top of a tram with an open vestibule. The old pub has been replaced by a modern brick house of Ansells brewery. To the left, Heathfield Road slants away, and to the right is the entrance to Barker Street. At top left, the distinctive rounded arch of the very popular Villa Cross cinema can be seen, which opened in 1912.

This service 24 tram is just setting off from Lozells to Colmore Row, via Wheeler Street. Note the Bundy clock. Between the edge of the tram and that of the pub can be seen part of the rounded top of the Villa Cross cinema. This scene dates from 7 September 1938.

A scene that suggests a bleak mid-winter day has arrived. After the hustle and bustle of Villa Cross, this seems a rather drab section of road, as were many in inner suburbs. But another busy and colourful shopping centre would soon be reached 'on the Lozells', as the saying went.

With the blinds drawn down above the pavement, this is obviously a sunny day. The right-hand shop is a 'Meat Purveyors', the 'B.A. Meat Co.' Next door Baines have popped up again, 'Noted for Pork Pies'. The adjoining building with the two handsome lamps is almost certainly a pub.

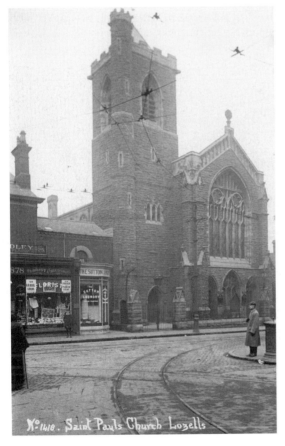

Above: Lozells enjoys fine weather again, at least on 'the sunny side of the street' – a phrase used by a popular song writer. Summery dresses are being worn by some of the ladies, but no one lacks a hat. Beneath the first sun blind on the right, Scott & Co. list some of their wares, including carpets and linoleum. Next door stands the Lozells Post Office. Woolworths, with their refreshing approach to retailing, 'nothing over sixpence', opened a branch 'on the Lozells' which was highly successful. This card was posted in 1924.

Left: Here stands a church with appropriate neighbours. At the bottom of the florists shop can be read 'Wreaths, bouquets ...' Cadbury are advertising in the side window. Postmarked 17 June 1914.

This busy junction, not least for trams, was photographed from all angles. The No.6 service car is dipping down into Birchfield Road, making for Perry Barr. The policeman looks watchfully towards the group of people outside the bank. 'Swan Vestas' was a brand of safety match designed for use by tobacco smokers, Vesta being the Roman goddess of hearth and household. This card was posted on 8 August 1914, four days after the start of the First World War.

At this point the No.5 service would have turned left into Slade Road in order to finish its journey. This No.2 tram, photographed in 1952 at Gravelly Hill, will be making for the city. Adverts on the wall reflect 'the march of time'. Foreign holidays are starting to become popular, as is television, but the real boom in the sales of both was still some time away. 'Spillers Shapes' were dog biscuits, always in steady demand.

Lodge Road formed a section of the route followed by service 32 from Foundry Road to Edmund Street. Lodge Road was part of the densely populated suburb of Winson Green, not unfairly known as a tough neighbourhood. A 1903 map (see next page) provides an insight into the 'hard times' nature of society with the welfare state nearly half a century distant. Lodge Road ran alongside a prison wall, the City Lunatic Asylum and City Fever Hospital. These formed part of a larger institutional complex including an infirmary and a workhouse. Various adverts can be seen on the card which was posted in 1910.

Lodge Road, nearly thirty years later. Fortunately, some of the institutions mentioned above have had their functions changed for the better and given less socially wounding titles.

104

8

SOME OTHER ROUTES OF 'YESTERDAY'

Navigation Street, at the rear of New Street Railway Station, had seen many trams come and go since it first became a terminus. This is a snapshot from April 1946, with a tramway official standing by the third car ready to give the tram the 'off'. The left-hand tram, service 33, travels to Ladywood. The next car, service 70, is for Rednal.

One of the services withdrawn before 1937 (replaced by buses) was the Navigation Street to Hagley Road, signed on the car along with 'Perfection Whisky'. Hagley Road, close to Edgbaston, the city's well-heeled suburb, was lined with fine, large Victorian and Edwardian houses. The card carries greetings to a son who is somewhere in 'Bowling Green, Ohio USA.' Only a one penny stamp has been affixed, but it has been franked 22 May 1915.

A card that was posted on 15 August 1914. Such an unusual fountain was not an everyday sight on a tram route – except this one! To the right runs Sandon Road with its own quota of large houses and gardens.

This photograph was taken from near the start of Hagley Road West looking across to the tram terminus at the Kings Head, one of the best-known hostelries in Birmingham. Years before, horse buses from New Street in the city centre had brought passengers to this point. To the left runs Bearwood Road, opposite Lordswood Road, another section of the Outer Circle bus route, in the direction of Harborne and Selly Oak – or the opposite direction.

Perhaps the most remarkable feature of this Nechells scene is the name of the road. Probably in few other thoroughfares in the city would residents have such a remote chance of hearing a cuckoo, living as they did near gas works and a sewage treatment plant. Many adverts make a reappearance.

Shrewd owners/managers turned this iconic pub to good account by alluding, above the door, to an incident in the English Civil War when Prince Rupert had used an earlier inn on this site as his temporary headquarters. The views of the urchins on the steps are not known.

This major arterial road was interspersed with rows of shops, as shown here. The corner shop is typical of many with its display of cigarette adverts, Players and Wills to the fore. Next door is The Hill School, perhaps with pupils collecting cigarette cards? The broad pavement is being neatly exploited by a motorist. (Stratford Road)

Further along the Stratford Road, in Hall Green, could be found this no-false-modesty shop display. The shaded lettering just above the seed adverts reads: 'Roberts – Forage contractors'. Clearly Scottish potatoes seem to enjoy a special status, six varieties being mentioned on the blackboard. It would be interesting to know if egg production was improved by Spratts Laymor.

This tram route through inner suburbs was relatively short. There is no mistaking the destination. Near to Small Heath Park, Byron Road formed part of a 'poetic' neighbourhood, as local roads included Waverley Road, Tennyson Road and Wordsworth Road. By contrast, Coventry Road, close by, sounded quite prosaic. The card was posted in 1917.

BIRMINGHAM F.C., 1926-7.

COPYRIGHT PHOTO
ALBERT WILKES, WEST BROMWICH

A. P. BROWN   BROWN   BOND   BOWDEN   OWEN   NEALE   HIBBS   WOOD   GARRATT   VINEY   MOORE
S. SCHOLEY (Trainer)   CROSBIE   STALEY   CASTLE   ASHURST   HARVEY   TREMELLING   BARTON   CRINGAN   WHARTON   W. KENDRICK (Assist. Trainer)
BRADFORD   BRUCE   DALE   JONES   BRIGGS   WOMACK   HARRIS   HUNTER   THIRLAWAY   LIDDELL   ISLIP
FIRTH   HAMBY   LESLIE   SMITH   RUSSELL   SCRIVEN

'Small Heath' conjures up, for older Brummies, memories of major manufacturers, the BSA, (Birmingham Small Arms Co.), the Singer Motor Works and, admittedly in a different league, St Andrews, home ground of the football club 'The Blues'. Memorable players include Hibbs, a very agile goalkeeper who played many times for England, and dashing centre forward, Bradford.

This service worked to one of the leafier suburbs, namely Hall Green, much sought after as a residential area. This photograph was taken in Highfield Road in 1936. The route was withdrawn the following January. One famous son of Hall Green was comedian Tony Hancock, and another was Nigel Mansell, giant of Formula 1 racing.

A slightly more commercial corner of Hall Green – damper too – is shown here. Even at this time it seems remarkable that until 1906 steam trams had run along this route as far as College Road. The route was first extended to the Bulls Head, and then again in 1928 to the city boundary at the Robin Hood Inn. The traffic island there was Birmingham's largest and became the butt of comedians' jokes.

A service 17 tram moves along High Street, Hall Green, on 2 January 1937, nearing the end of its work on this route. The nearby shop, looking like a converted house, advertises 'Wallpaper Stores' and 'Timber Yard', which helps to explain the appearance of the front garden. The PATCH on the tram refers to the *Evening Dispatch*, a Birmingham newspaper.

This marks the end of the line in a double sense; the end of the route and of the service. Starting at 12.00 a.m., the six ways to which reference is made on the card constitute Shirley Road, Solihull Lane, Stratford Road, Baldwins Lane, Robin Hood Lane and Stratford Road again. (Hall Green)

On 6 September 1917 Maud writes: 'My dear Lizzie, Sorry you all had to get up for German visitors...'
Presumably this is a reference to an air raid on London during the First World War, Lizzie living in E.17.
Kings Heath, once a village and formerly part of Kings Norton, became another attractive residential
area. The tram is signed 'Alcester Lane to Hill Street'.

Yardley, once in Worcestershire, was also 'recruited' into Birmingham, Warwickshire. Under a light
sprinkling of snow, the scene focuses not only on a tram but another tram terminus, the well-known
Swan Hotel. On this route trams were replaced by trolley buses. Yardley also became a popular residential
outer suburb.

This is one of many postcards depicting the affectionately remembered Bull Ring of the first half of the last century. St Martin's Church stands dignified and untroubled by the surrounding hubbub. So does the statue of Nelson 'presiding' over the raucous buying and selling around the open-air stalls. Trams are moving to and away from Moor Street, indifferent to the workmen grouped by their temporary shelter. Hemmed in by four boards, the sandwich-board man advertises 'Browns Gents Boots Special Sale This Week' outside Mr Browns.

'Seen as well as heard the news?' After an earlier life as an ordinary cinema, in 1932 this news theatre (a city High Street cinema) was the first of its kind to open in the provinces. A Washwood Heath tram makes its way up to its terminus in Martineau Street. 'Come on, let's go and see a great cartoon and a travelogue about Hawaii.'

9

THE WAY THINGS WERE

There would be much to mourn in the passing of the tramways. But cyclists would be relieved that the danger of slipping into a tramline, thereby causing a fall, would be gone. For safety, tramlines should be crossed by cyclists at right angles, as above. The hazard mentioned was well illustrated on a cigarette card, one of a series on 'Safety First' issued by Wills. (See p.126)

Royal visits and royal occasions such as coronations gave trams opportunities to shine. This particular coronation was that of King George V and Queen Mary.

The purpose of this special car is not self evident. The car itself is of the latest design, and the city's last new tram, in service from 1930. All the passengers and staff appear to be men, most of them youthful. The notice in the window, Rednal and Dudley, suggests a trip to the Lickeys and the new Dudley Zoo. Could they be a group of tram buffs?

A photograph that was taken on 17 June 1951 at the Navigation Street terminus. There is a touch of irony here, with the presence, right, of the Birmingham Garage, for it was the internal combustion engine, in its bus form, that put paid to the tramway system in 1953. Incidentally, Car No.842 was one of 'two experimental lightweight aluminium bodied trams' that entered service in 1929, designed to seat sixty-three passengers.

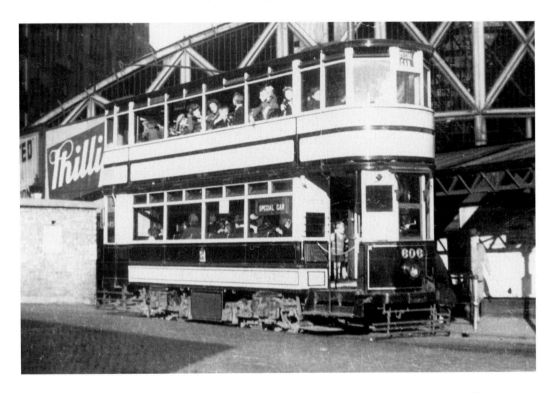

It is not too fanciful to suppose that the young boy in short trousers is saying something like, ''ow fast does it go mister?' From the appearance of the passengers, this could be an outing for youngsters under adult supervision. When the photograph was taken on 7 July 1945, the war in Europe had been over for a couple of months.

On occasion, even a special royal tram had to share a shed with run-of-the-mill neighbours! Such illuminated trams were very popular with the public who turned out in large numbers along the routes prescribed for them.

Returning to the every-day humdrum, this is the upper saloon of Car No.668 on 28 June 1953, shortly before the tram system finally closed down. Attempts were already being made to establish a legacy, this card being sold 'To Aid Tramcar Preservation'.

BIRMINGHAM TRAMWAYS GAZETTE

*The Official Magazine of the Birmingham Corporation Tramway
and Omnibus Department Social, Athletic & Thrift Society.*

VOL. 11. No. 3.   AUGUST, 1934.   Honorary Editor: FREDK. GEO HOPTON   ONE PENNY

CONTENTS

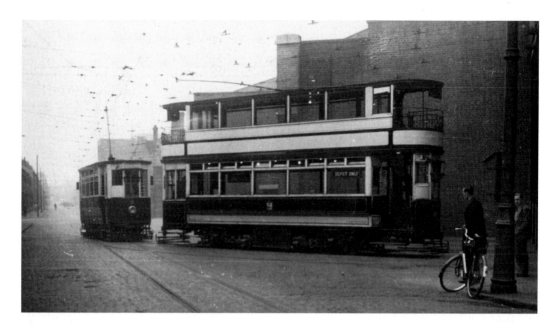

Miller Street Depot was located in Hockley. For a variety of reasons single-decker trams were not used in any major way, although for a time they proved their worth on the Aston route until a railway bridge was raised sufficiently to allow the passage, if only just, of double-deckers. Experiments were also carried out using them as unpowered trailers, but with limited success.

'Depot Only' was a sign unwelcome to would-be passengers as it meant that they could not board the tram. On the left can be seen the front of the still sturdy shell of the city's Market Hall. The tram has just emerged from Moor Street. Oswald Bailey Ltd was a kind of army surplus store, and Hobbies sold material and tools for fretwork, a very popular hobby between the wars.

This photograph of Rosebery Street Depot was taken on 29 March 1939. By this time only the 87 service of the four 80s shown was still operating, from Edmund Street to Dudley. In effect, this is a souvenir card for the staff and other interested parties.

This is another card in the same vein of sentiment. Apparently the photograph was taken at 2.00 a.m. on 6 January 1937 at Highgate Road Depot, following the closure of tram services for Stratford Road. Route indicators have been turned to show the numbers of routes formerly worked from the depot.

Nostalgic record keeping did not remove the need for continuing hard work in the maintenance and repair of those trams still in business. This is a scene from the Kyotts Lake Road Depot. The tram advertising DREFT (thought to be a detergent) may need more than a wash and polish.

This shows a single-decker waiting for...? Among the reasons for their limited use as trailers were the results of experiments carried out in 1917 which showed that track alterations would be needed, and, given the shortage of materials in wartime, such changes were not feasible.

Many postcards were published of the 1907 fatal tram crash in Warstone Lane in the early days of electric trams. Two such cards appear in Volume I. The details of the above crash are not known to the author except that the accident occurred on 26 June 1916 by Soho Road Railway Station. Apparently it was a South Staffs car.

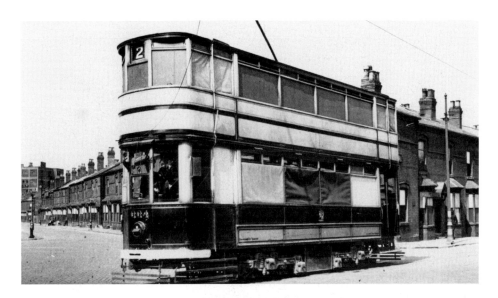

During the Second World War, when air raids threatened, in order to reduce the risk of concentrated damage to trams in their depots, cars were sometimes dispersed to outdoor tracks. Even so, forty-one trams were destroyed and many more damaged. Track and overhead wiring suffered damage and bomb blast shattered many tram windows. There was much to repair, but materials, even glass, were in short supply. Fortunately, improvisation had not become a casualty!

Is this the tram equivalent of the elephants' graveyard, which few people know about? During the lifespan of the Corporation's tram system, the city bought and managed 843 cars. Shown here is a scrapyard at Stratford-on-Avon.

Could this be a tram version of the walking wounded? It is not a lamentable attempt at camouflage but evidence of wartime shortages – in this case of paint – yellow and blue. This car and its passengers, outside Birchfield Picture House, Perry Barr, had to be content with battleship grey.

work. The answer was simply nothing beyond the rich satisfaction of realising that something had been accomplished to save a fellow-being. The public, however, did not realise the very great amount of self-sacrificing endeavours made on their behalf by the members, who, he was pleased to say, were increasing in numbers. The Chief Commissioner was thanked by the County Commissioner, on whose call the parade gave resounding cheers.

Owing to lack of support, the proposed outing to Matlock on September 9th, will not take place.

Dr. Burges will commence a new series of lectures in first-aid on Sunday, September 2nd. All old members are requested to attend. New members will be specially welcome.

E. WORRALL.

Billiards & Snooker

(Outstanding matches having been at last contested, final figures are now available.)

BILLIARDS LEAGUE.

Division "B."

	P.	W.	L.	Pts.
Tennant Street	80	55	25	55
Highgate Road	80	48	32	48
Cotteridge	80	46	34	46
West Smethwick	80	45	35	45
Buildings	80	34	46	34
Head Office	65	29	36	29
Rosebery Street	70	27	43	27
Selly Oak	60	26	34	26
Tyburn Road	70	23	47	23

SNOOKER LEAGUE.

Division "A."

	P.	W.	L.	Pts.
	00	69	31	69
	00	67	33	67
	00	62	38	62
	00	61	39	61
	95	47	48	47
	90	44	46	44
	95	44	51	44
	00	44	56	44
	95	28	67	28
	90	20	70	20

W. H. LAW.

BOWLS LEAGUE TABLES.

Division "A."

	P.	W.	L.	For	Against	Pts.
Highgate Road	7	7	0	686	440	14
Acocks Green	8	7	1	779	548	14
Rosebery Street	7	5	2	644	558	10
Washwood Heath	8	5	3	689	648	10
Kyotts Lake Road	7	4	3	606	546	8
West Smethwick	8	4	4	685	702	8
Permanent Way	6	3	3	491	495	6
Arthur Street	6	0	6	390	587	0
Overhead	7	0	7	406	725	0
Selly Oak	4	0	4	297	384	0

Division "B."

	P.	W.	L.	For	Against	Pts.
Hockley	8	8	0	739	458	16
Miller Street	7	7	0	692	450	14
Harborne	4	4	0	410	254	8
Tyburn Road	6	4	2	563	452	8
Moseley Road	6	4	2	537	489	8
Cotteridge	8	4	4	648	650	8
Tennant Street	6	2	4	502	450	4
Perry Barr	7	1	6	439	642	2
Witton	4	0	4	239	399	0
Barford Street	5	0	5	344	504	0
Buildings	7	0	7	362	717	0

W. H. LAW.

Male Voice Choir Notes

Since my last notes our membership has increased, but there is still room for new members, particularly from Perry Barr and Selly Oak. Can we announce next month that every Branch of the Society is represented in our ranks?

We have moved our place of practice to the King's Arms (at the corner of Suffolk Street and Station Street). During our stay at the Tramways Club we have received much help and every consideration from the Steward and his staff.

The Quartette entered the Bournville Musical Festival and obtained third place—a splendid achievement. The test piece was "Here's a Health unto his Majesty." (A subtle choice for Bournville.—Ed.)

We should like it known that any member of the Social Club may come along and join the Choir. Should a man wish to rehearse any new song for his own benefit, our talented pianist, Mr. Woods, will gladly render him every assistance.

JAMES CONLON.

Angling News

The contest fished at Bushley, on Sunday, July 22nd, 1934, was favoured with brilliant weather. One hundred and forty-four members enjoyed themselves for sport was good.

The winner proved to be Mr. W. Faulkner, of Harborne Branch, who weighed in a very good catch.

The awards were:—

	£	s.	d.
1. W. Faulkner, Harborne	3	3	0
2. W. Perry, Hockley	2	2	0
3. J. S. Wood, Washwood Heath	1	5	0
4. A. Read, Miller Street	1	2	6
5. H. Harris, Overhead	1	2	6
6. H. T. Miles, Selly Oak	1	0	0
7. H. Roberts, Harborne	1	0	0
8. R. Lewis, Highgate Road		17	6
9. E. Scrivens, Arthur Street		17	6
10. B. Ravenhill, Perry Barr		15	0
11. W. Vale, Tyburn Road		15	0
12. H. Faulkner, Hockley		12	6
13. F. Byford, Moseley Road		12	6
14. W. Smith, Perry Barr		10	0

15 to 26: Messrs. J. Rollason, Overhead; E. Burgess, Washwood Heath; R. Wilson, Permanent Way; J. Meir, Arthur Street; W. Coron, Hockley; E. Bradley, Hockley; E. Millward, Acocks Green; T. Cross, Acocks Green; F. Ansell, Perry Barr; E. Teague, Cotteridge; G. Anderson, Rosebery Street; and F. Hopkins, Hockley.

The special prize for the competitor landing the heaviest fish went to Mr. A. Read, of Miller Street, with 2 lbs. 11 ozs. 3 drams.

The Social Club Contest, open to all employees, will be held at Twyning, on Sunday, 26th August, 1934. 'Buses will leave Navigation Street at 7 a.m., and the Three Hour Contest will commence at soon as possible after 10 a.m.

Important.—All members must be licensed before the Contest commences.

Prize money to the value of not less than Twenty Pounds will be given. The 'buses will return as required, the actual times to be announced on the day of the Contest.

The 'bus fare is three shillings and nine-pence. Every competitor on the vehicles must be in possession of a travelling permit.

Branch representatives must make early application for the permits, and not later than 20th August. All applications must be accompanied by the travelling money and one shilling for the Pool.

Swimming Splashes

The Society's Gold Medal for swimming 440 yards under seven minutes has been won by Mr. F. Woodward, of Acocks Green Branch, who is to be heartily congratulated on being the first member to obtain it. The same swimmer and J. Lock, of Perry Barr, have won the Society's Silver Medal for swimming the same distance (440 yards), in under ten minutes.

Times:—

F. Woodward, 7 minutes 47 3/5 secs.
J. Lock, 9 minutes 57 2/5 secs.

Mr. A. Allbut, of Tyburn Road, has made two unsuccessful attempts for the gold medal, on the last occasion missing the honour by only twenty seconds.

In the Business Houses' team race we were defeated by the Municipal S.C. and the Dunlop S.C. Our representatives were Messrs. Butler (Harborne), Bell (Head Office), O'Neil (Miller Street), and Woodward (Acocks Green). The events were closely contested.

Several promising swimmers are making good progress under Professor Dugmore, who has been appointed swimming instructor to the Society. The Annual Swimming Gala will, in consequence, carry an added interest. The date of this event is September 25th.

A two lengths members' handicap will take place at the Moseley Road Baths, on Friday, August 25th, at 8 p.m.

It has been suggested that a Swimming Supper and Concert be arranged. Will Branch representatives get into touch with their members and see if there is any chance of the idea being carried to a successful conclusion?

Friendly water polo matches with the Dunlop S.C. and Municipal S.C. will be played on August 20th and 31st respectively.

D. HARDY.

Right: 'Only a couple of days to go now.' Could that be what the conductress is saying as the photographer records this scene? A photograph from 2 July 1953, three days before the last tram made its exit.

Below: Local dignitaries, well wrapped up, celebrate the dawn of a new transport age. Erdington 1907.

Forty-six years later, on 5 July 1953, Brummies in their thousands crowd pavements to pay cheering tribute to the city's last tram working its way to the final terminus. As the inscription reads, 'Well done old timer'.

This card was franked on 23 October 1915. Ladies are now replacing tram conductors serving in the forces, many of whom are no doubt Tommies in the trenches. While there are many adverts to study, the cheerful smiles of the girls are far more attractive.

Other titles published by The History Press

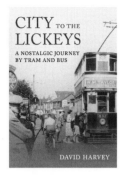

City to the Lickeys: A Nostalgic Journey by Tram and Bus
DAVID HARVEY

For many hardworking Brummies a day trip to the Lickey Hills was their only entertainment or leisure activity. From the spring of 1924 until the mid-1950s, a trip there on the Rednal tram for a 5d ticket became the only holiday many people could afford. Take a journey along Bristol Road and Pershore Road from the city centre to Rednal and Rubery and to Cotteridge by tram and bus; look at the street scenes from a different time and see why the Lickey Hills became such an attraction.

ISBN 978 0 7524 4697 4

Top-Deck Travel: A History of Britain's Open-Top Buses
PHILIP C. MILES

This illustrated history charts the development of the open-top bus, from the early 1900s when buses ordinarily had an open top-deck to the bustling sightseeing operations so popular around the world today, recalling many operators along the way who have since been relegated to the annals of history.

ISBN 978 0 7524 5137 4

Luton Corporation Transport
PETER ROSE

Covering the history of municipal transport in Luton from the first horse-drawn buses and the town's electric trams through to the sale of the undertaking to United Counties, the bus company which dominated services in the rest of Bedfordshire, this fully illustrated book will have a nostalgic appeal to all who have lived and worked in Luton during the Corporation era and beyond to many bus enthusiasts nationwide.

ISBN 978 0 7524 4913 5

The London Bus Story
JOHN CHRISTOPHER

Buses have been operating on London's streets since 1829, originally with horse-drawn omnibuses, and the London Omnibus Co. was founded in 1855 to regulate the various services. More recent innovations such as the 'bendy' bus have not been popular, but today the practicality of pushchair and wheelchair access has consigned the Routemaster to a nostalgic, but much-loved, position.

ISBN 978 0 7524 5084 1

Visit our website and discover thousands of other History Press books.

www.thehistorypress.co.uk